W9-BCF-320

SACRED LIES AND SILENCES

A Psychology of Religious Disguise

Vernon Ruland, S.J.

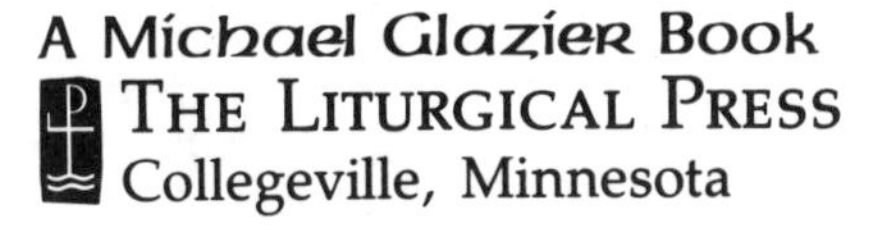
A Michael Glazier Book
THE LITURGICAL PRESS
Collegeville, Minnesota

200.19
R

A Michael Glazier Book published by The Liturgical Press

Cover design by Greg Becker

© 1994 by The Order of St. Benedict, Inc., Collegeville, Minnesota. All rights reserved. No part of this book may be reproduced in any form or by any means, electronic or mechanical, including photocopying, recording, taping, or any retrieval system, without the written permission of The Liturgical Press, Collegeville, Minnesota 56321.

Published in the United States of America

1 2 3 4 5 6 7 8 9

Library of Congress Cataloging-in-Publication Data

Ruland, Vernon.
Sacred lies and silences : a psychology of religious disguise / Vernon Ruland.
p. cm.
"A Michael Glazier book."
Includes bibliographical references and index.
ISBN 0-8146-5847-4
1. Psychology, Religious. 2. Spirituality. 3. Individual differences—Religious aspects.
BL53.R835 1994
200'.1'9—dc20 93-34712
CIP

Contents

Preface

My title and subtitle suggest the principal theme. Appearances often mislead. Mere husks of religion can be disguised by a pious lie, or the deepest religious vision disguised by a modest silence. For the inner life may prove now less, now more religious than first appears. My focus is the balanced spiritual human person, and the range of distortions, both psychological and religious, prompted whenever this integration is threatened. At a quick glance, the cast of characters may give an impression of some lurid tabloid: cult victims, civil dissenters, televangelists, fundamentalist crusaders, the paranoid and guilt-ridden, prophets and gurus and holy fools. However, the mood of this study is mostly tolerant and constructive. It tries to mediate some of the collisions between cultures, between academic disciplines, and between religious traditions.

This book revises the longstanding agenda and ground rules for dialogue between psychotherapists and pastoral theologians. Stock contenders were once just an agnostic psychoanalyst, and a priest, minister, or rabbi. But now the therapeutic component is widened to embrace a huge spectrum of therapies, both East and West, pre-Freud and post-Freud, and the fluid borders where psychology tapers off into sociology and anthropology. The religious component expands, too, to include every major world faith, the universal religious dimension in human history, and its unique, often disguised realization in each individual.

A brief outline of these eight chapters may prove helpful. Chapter 1 defines the inclusive religious factor, and surveys a range of its most common disguises. The disguise may function as either alias or counterfeit—the first implying silence and anonymity, the second lies or other disparities. Chapters 1 to 3 select a few misleading aliases for deeper study, notably conscience, the religionless outsider, and the realm of magic, ghosts, and demons. Chapter 4 finds religious traces even at the extremity of mental disorder, especially among schizophrenics.

After an introduction in the last pages of chapter 4 to more widespread disorders or counterfeits, the next three chapters explore the three classical Sacred Ways—a spirituality of action, of affectivity, and of contemplation. Chapters 5 to 7 each sketch the mature spiritual ideal first, then its potential distortions. Representative counterfeits include religious paranoia, guilt, co-dependency, self-effacement, and solipsism. Chapter 8, shifting attention from the person healed to the healer, uncovers traces of empathy and crypto-religious purpose in all effective therapists. To be comprehensive, the healer must draw upon distinct traditions of the shaman, priest, and psychotherapist.

My guiding methodology is laid bare in chapter 1 and in the introductions to both chapters 2 and 3. The genre of this book is an extended informal essay, in the inclusive interdisciplinary manner of Freud, Jung, Fromm, or Rollo May. Though given explicit permission on occasion to write up a case study from my work as therapist, such as the sustained narrative that concludes chapter 3, I always doctor up inessential details in client and student case material to protect confidentiality. My illustrations are drawn from the perennial classics of literature, from years of teaching, counseling, and pastoral experience, and from scrutiny of my own inner world or the lives of those nearby. These examples must be taken as evocative, of course, not strictly probative. For "hard" experimental data supporting a specific psychological theory, readers will want to check the research listed in my footnotes at the end of the book.

This book is an urgent follow-up to *Eight Sacred Horizons: The Religious Imagination East and West* (Macmillan, 1985), which gauged how it feels in the pulse to believe and pray within cultures and spiritualities other than one's own. There I aimed for informed empathy rather than assessment. However, there are millions of religious people living outside the boundaries of these eight extant traditions. And more important, an official portrait of Hindu or Christian spirituality, for instance, must always be checked out against its living exponents—against actual religious attitudes recorded in popular literature, iconography, or biography, and interpreted by psychology, anthropology, and the other human sciences. My earlier book scarcely hinted at the ingenious ways some people conceal their loftiest ideals, whereas others betray ideals by selective inattention or the parody of inflexible pursuit.

Though my own spiritual odyssey does not figure in the present book directly, a few of its unexpected zigzags ought to be mentioned. They help explain both the breadth and the limitations of culture, training, and religious perspective in my material. After becoming a Jesuit priest, I first headed for graduate studies in English, but the stimulating *aggiornamento* milieu of the sixties within my own Church enticed me toward a doctorate in religion and literature from the University of Chicago's Protestant divinity school. Another sudden reversal occurred a few years later in Detroit, as the Vietnam War intruded with increasing menace upon my career as a university professor. When not teaching, I became a draft counselor, and studied for a master's in counseling to offer more skillful support for conscientious objectors.

A third significant detour came later in San Francisco, through my work as a state-licensed marriage and family counselor. For I now found myself teacher and mentor to a large number of international students on the Pacific Rim. And as a resident priest in student dorms, I became neighbor to a wide ethnic spectrum of dialect, dress, music, and aromas from portable hotplates. I soon recognized the need to take soundings in religious traditions other than my own Christian heritage, and within a few years most of my teaching and writing centered upon this new search.

All three of these reversals make their way into the pages that follow: a committed but self-questioning spirituality, an interest in people, trust that the sacred must be present somehow in each conscientious human quest and decision, an enjoyment of literature and myth, and an eagerness to teach, write, and counsel.

I am grateful to three close friends for encouragement and feedback on this manuscript: Fr. Paul Bernadicou, S.J., associate professor of religious studies at the University of San Francisco; and my former students Dr. Christopher Hayward, assistant professor of psychiatry at Stanford University Medical Center, and David McSpadden, teacher of mathematics at the Stuart Hall School for Boys. Throughout my research the USF Gleeson Library staff have given cordial and reliable assistance. At meals each day with Jesuit colleagues, I would often try out a half-formulated insight or ask about some biblical concept, a French spelling, or an Hasidic parable.

I now pay renewed tribute to a diffuse communal network, anonymous and largehearted, that underwrites what is often mistaken for just a solo performance. Thus, I acknowledge the many people that stand behind my present work—therapy clients especially, family and friends, students from many nations, and a providential line of teachers and counselors and spiritual directors, whose wisdom and example have helped shape my life. To them all I dedicate this book, an attempt to fathom and etch on stone my own varieties of religious experience.

1

Sacred Disguises: The Alias and the Counterfeit

Any psychology of religious experience ought to begin by exploring a basic ambiguity that undercuts all surveys and conjectures. This can be summed up in two brief truisms. Granted that many people are just what they seem, some prove far more religious than they appear. And second, some prove far less religious than they appear.

The first scenario offers surprising new depths. For instance, beneath a modest secular death "for others," you can sometimes detect a vital spiritual impulse, groping to push aside or even reclaim traditional religious words. Though my Irish cousins interject "Glory be to God" and "Sweet Mother Mary" into every few lines of smalltalk, most other friends prefer respectful disuse, rather than misuse or overuse of sacred names. Brave Doctor Rieux in Camus' *The Plague* has no interest in the tired vocabulary of heroism, sanctity, or God. He asks only to heal and become a genuine human being.

My Japanese friend Norieko, quick to distance herself from patterns of church attendance, bedtime and table prayers, or the religion shelf in bookstores, first introduced herself to me as someone of no *shukyo,* without a religion. After more patient listening, I realized she identifies with no institutional religion, yet acknowledges *shukyo shin,* a true religious heart and feeling. In another example, Robert Lowell, appraising his career as a poet, once noted that explicit religious symbols pervading the early books had almost disappeared in his later work. Yet he judged the recent poems more genuinely religious. Embedded in situations like these, the spiritual framework hides itself in a silence that is all ears, and ripe with promise. As an anonymous spirituality, it picks up some plausible disguise, which I shall call a religious *alias.*

The second of the two truisms above cautions that people may prove less religious than they seem. You soon learn the patronizing smile of those too sure they're saved, the alms bestowed with scarcely suppressed disdain, a predatory fever to manipulate other spiritual lives. Recent TV screens have played up pedophilia in the sacristy, televangelist fraud and fornication, and expedient prison conversions of ex-politicians. The surface creed of some people may freeze to dogmatism, their worship to ritualism, their ethics to legalism. Prophets in all religious traditions, almost by job description, are those chosen to smoke out such distortions, and winnow the authentic tao, dharma, or godhead. This facade of lies will be called a religious *counterfeit*.

Like any other forgery, the religious sort implies a mismatch, calculated or unconscious, between face value and true worth. A motive nominally religious may give way to a style of life undermining or caricaturing that motive. As Kierkegaard says, even the truth can become a lie on the lips of some people. Though the religious factor withstands easy definition, many religious counterfeits can be detected quickly—easier, of course, in others than in oneself—long before the exact strategy of pretense can be understood.

Before attempting to pin down distortions, however, it is wise to determine exactly what is being distorted. The religious phenomenon itself must be mapped out and redefined, now and in chapters 2 and 3. The rest of this present chapter will analyze the elusive religious alias, the basis for its opacity, and its place at the center of a mature human personality.

The Religious Factor

By the religious factor I mean whatever explicit or partially conscious drive, credo, or value system lies at the root of behavior marked by awe, commitment, ecstasy, and moral seriousness. The ideal religious person or society is one living, more or less, a religiously integrated existence. In this model situation the adjective *religious* and the adverb *religiously* would be so pervasive that no sector of life could be readily compartmentalized into the noun *religion*. A religious quality would permeate that life, as the center from which everything else derives its meaning, or without which all else would be meaningless. Or reversing this principle, if you could probe underneath daily behavior and values and language to find that which ultimately underlies the life of a people or an individual, you would call this source religious.[1]

As an indispensable premise to the pages that follow, this explanation deserves hard scrutiny. Like any other definition, whether from

Webster's or custom-built, it opts for an abridged theory, arguing its own claim to coherence and applicability.

Three major ingredients in the definition stand out. The first has already been implied—sensitivity to the hidden religious dynamic and wariness about obvious labels. One standard survey question reads: "Do you have, practice, or belong to a religion?" My Japanese friend Norieko's negative response to this question has been mentioned, acknowledging not a religion but religious feelings. Thus, her entire spiritual style and existence must be taken into account, not just an inventory of her sacred words or tokens of membership. Whether her life is religious or not is almost beyond proof. You can only measure how closely her self-perceived religious identity is integrated with her own characteristic motives and behavior. Religiously Norieko is more or less genuine—or conversely, if you will, more or less counterfeit.

The second component in this theory is a bias toward continuity. However, it is often the discontinuity or disparity between substantive religion and ordinary life that rivets the attention of prophets and theologians. Yearning for an apocalyptic clarity, some minds divide sacred and profane sharply and rule out any fuzzy overlap between them. Others labor to single out this pervasive religious quality, and segregate it from dilution or displacement. You can understand, too, why an average TV crew, assigned to film religious life in a Navajo community, for instance, tend to overlook the intangible spirituality animating each family's routine hospitality and work. Instead cameras pounce upon the overt religious symbol: a picturesque sweat lodge, grandfather's chanted morning prayer, the daughter's initiation rites into puberty.

Yet the more inward, silent continuities between sacred and profane are exactly what this present chapter intends to reinstate. At first, locating the religious phenomenon almost everywhere looks suspiciously like locating it nowhere. But devout Hasidic Jews find even the study of mathematics an act of worship. An Australian aborigine links sacred originating forces "once upon a time" with every meaningful act performed in the present, whether hunting, mating, or sleeping. Zen enlightenment means being intensely present in each commonplace event—when you're drinking tea, nothing is more important than drinking tea. Sociologist Georg Simmel points to the ceremonial reverence that permeates Confucian family and work relationships, and especially the blend of moral, religious, and juridical sanctions in Hindu *dharma*, Greek *themis*, and Latin *fas*. Similar to my own approach, his theory treats the religious factor as a heightening and completion of all other human facets.[2]

As an immediate corollary to this continuity principle, the third ingredient in my definition presumes coherence between the religious factor and a mature personality. In other words, the conventional dichotomy between sacred and profane ought to be reinterpreted as a yin-yang complementary duality. Two polarities without conflict, Spirit and Psyche, religious growth and psychological growth, are distinct but inseparable components in human life, each needing the other for completeness.

What has just been stated about religious wholeness or integration will pass today for a commonplace of New Age Spirituality or the Human Potential Movement. Yet its controversial impact can be grasped more vividly, if set beside its militant antithesis, a manifesto two decades ago by Albert Ellis, founder of rational-emotive therapy. Starting with a contentious definition of religion as "faith unfounded on fact, or dependency on some assumed superhuman entities," he selects only those cases I would diagnose as religious disorders. Each of the clients he labels "religionist" turns out rigid, fanatical, dependent, or authoritarian. In another matching column Ellis offers a checklist of mature human endowments: self-interest, self-direction, tolerance, the acceptance of uncertainty, flexibility, scientific thinking, commitment, risk-taking, self-acceptance. But each described feature is narrowed in such a way that self-direction excludes other-direction, and knowledge, based on the strict experimental science model, excludes the least glimmer of transcendence.[3]

There can be no possible rapprochement, then, between religion and psychological maturity as Ellis conceives them. He calls for an aggressive sort of therapist, geared to smoke out and eliminate the client's religious values. Such a model clashes directly with my own inclusive therapy ideal, to be explored in chapter 8—the healer trained to challenge and nourish a mature spirituality.

The Alias and Its Implications

Though further dialogue between the Ellis approach and my own might prove insightful, our two contrasting worldviews dramatize right away how the scope in each interpreter shapes what is interpreted. Many psychological attitudes that he judges mature, I judge immature. Religious behavior that he thinks characteristic, I think scarcely worthy of the name. Our contrast in theory stems from two unique milieus, character styles, and differing contacts with disturbed or balanced religious people. In later chapters it will be important to clarify and tighten whatever criteria can be devised for discerning a counterfeit. And this category must include, not just the counterfeit religious, but especially, the counterfeit psychologically mature.

Thus, you may choose to constrict the religious perimeter just to include behavior that is odd, irrational, and unbalanced. But then you can be expected to chart a huge swath outside the perimeter somehow, a realm of mature values now reconstituted as nonreligious. For Ellis, this wise alternative is called a "non-supernatural philosophy of life or a code of ethics." For Freud, dismissing all religious experience as a neurotic sidetrack or throwback, the biblical god-image is replaced by "our god Logos," or with more accuracy, Plato's Eros. More popular contemporary alternatives come to mind—triumphant modern science, cosmological myths of entropy or evolutionary progress, Mother Earth and a new Puritan ethic of anti-pollution. Abandoning a strict Catholic or Muslim tradition, for example, you may turn to the Communist Party, Greenpeace, a twelve-step recovery program, or some other secular ideology, still organizing the whole of life, from dawn to bedtime, around a crypto-religious vision.

Now all that has been consigned to this rich expanding domain of nonreligious or quasi-religious significance, I am determined to annex back within borders of the inclusive religious factor defined above. Each of these imaginative alternatives shall be reappropriated as a potential religious alias. There are two major advantages in viewing the religious factor and its equivalents in so comprehensive a manner.

First, a multitude of religious aliases now shift into view. Faith, political commitment, sexual life-style, or the ethos of an entire era or civilization—each is rendered coherent by psychological maneuvers that show arresting parallels. New unlikely affiliations occur. It becomes obvious how a filter of language, logic, and unquestioned assumptions in a particular culture or time can edit out the very impulse to name a religious experience. Prime Minister Nehru of India, for instance, detesting the bigotry, exploitation, and blindness he had long associated with local Hindu and Muslim sectarians, felt compelled to identify his own humanist faith not as a religion, but a spirituality. In a comparable way, Nobel Prize novelist Nadine Gordimer, though describing herself as an atheist, adds a wise proviso. She admits a profoundly religious temperament, and "perhaps, brought up differently in a different milieu, in a different way, I might have been a religious person."[4]

Religious visibility is now flaunted, now disguised, depending on prevailing legal attitudes. In the United States, some groups today reject the legitimation that others crave. In recent years, the Church of

Scientology has been soliciting academic support, including my own, to solidify its claim as a true religion, and thus entitled to tax exemption. Yet in New Jersey, Transcendental Meditation advocates lost a case trying to prove themselves not a religion. Members wanted to introduce mind techniques into public school curricula without violating First Amendment cautions against religious favoritism.

The second advantage to this inclusive religious approach is its flexible calculus, adjusting to people's words and concepts mostly within their own ultimate frame of reference. For what makes activities like tea-drinking and study a religious activity can only be determined according to that specific worldview, not by the outsider's a priori categories of religious and nonreligious. Each religious manifestation within a culture is embedded in a unique world of actual work and social patterns. This is true, even more so, in the microcosm of an individual life.

The contrast between a misconstrued alias, and the individual's actual religious alias can be illustrated in two vivid situations. If assigned, for instance, to draw up an index for Annie Dillard's autobiography, *An American Childhood,* readers might paste an impulsive religious label on three Church-related scenarios in the book. These events comprise a fervent Bible camp experience in childhood, an unresolved discussion with her Presbyterian minister on the problem of evil, and her critique of a bored, hypocritical congregation during one Sunday service.

Yet these impromptu labels pinned on Dillard's text would have missed the diffuse spiritual wonder, her Thoreau-like excitement over books, rocks, a chemistry set, an insect collection, and every natural miracle uncovered in nearby Frick Park. She begins to see the prosaic surface of Pittsburgh as a geode, concealing under its dull surface an invisible city with underground corridors of agate, moonstone, and blue azulite. How could anyone compute the pages that register this permeating visionary dimension in her life? Yet it is no less religious than the explicit moments associated with her Church community. In fact, this dimension is probably more religious, for it stands as her own unique alias. "There was no corner of my brain," she says, "where you couldn't find, among the files of clothing labels and heaps of rocks, among the swarms of protozoans and shelves of novels, whole tapes and snarls and reels of Bible."[5]

My second example of the misconstrued religious factor is based on a stormy conference with two people a few years ago, she a Reform Jew, he a Roman Catholic, whom I shall call Miriam and Kevin. Both were anxious to strike some compromise between their two colliding religious traditions before getting married. An initial obstacle was the demand by Kevin and his family, not only for a traditional Catholic wedding, but for Miriam's prior conversion. This move prompted her own family's counter-demand for Kevin's conversion to Judaism. Neither family would hear of one interfaith ceremony, or two ceremonies in succession. Miriam and Kevin each hoped to convert the other. Each counted on a uniform faith as the stable basis for their love, and also for rearing a family.

The first to yield ground in this contest was Miriam, badgered by Kevin to admit that Jewish ethnic identity, not Jewish religious belief and ritual, were all that had ever mattered to her parents and herself. Yet even before she mentioned possibly becoming a Catholic, I urged this pivotal decision be deferred till much later, after the marriage. Unwarranted pressures from Kevin's family, a sincere eagerness to please and identify with Kevin, almost no time to reflect—these factors could only undermine the chances for a mature religious choice now. But at this juncture in the conversation, Kevin himself, disarmed by Miriam's honest readiness to submit, had to confess with embarrassment his own diffidence about the Catholic tradition. He had not been a conventional practicing Catholic since adolescence, nor did he ever expect to become active.

Cut adrift from both family traditions, then, where could both of them locate that uniform religious foundation which meant so much to them? Somewhat downcast, Miriam began to dredge up words to match the crucial values that bound them together in practice. There were honesty and kindness, respect for other people, hard work, a sense of humor and flexibility, the importance of individual conscience, innovative attitudes toward educating their children. These were matters they often discussed, each tolerating whatever differences arose between them. Both mentioned praying alone sometimes to a personal God. A few weeks after this conference, to the dismay of both families, the couple settled for a quiet civil marriage at city hall. Their Synagogue and Church, the family and society around them, their priest counselor, even Miriam and Kevin—all of us had acquiesced in two unexamined, misleading self-definitions. Meanwhile, an overlooked religious alias had long been uniting them.

Case Study: The Alias of Conscience

Various widespread religious aliases were mentioned before, such as the myth of an uncontaminated Mother Earth or of a scientific millennium. However, in political campaigns, managerial boardrooms, and the courts, there is one alias more prevalent still, which now merits attention. This is the weasel word *conscience.* The term means a sense of moral accountability toward God, or toward the sacred center that gives underlying coherence to each individual life.

Any serious shift in the public consensus tends at length to surface in some major court decision, with consequences that require candid legal and moral appraisal. As the ensuing case study will show, the U.S. Supreme Court mirrors a recent, and I think commendable, change in public attitudes toward the sincere conscientious objector. It is instructive to watch the court stretching conventional definitions of religious identity in order to make room for the dissenting conscience.

To understand the court's religious position, it may help to draw upon my own perceptions as a volunteer draft counselor after 1965. That year marked two momentous events. There was first the promulgation of Second Vatican Council documents, signed by the pope and all Catholic bishops convening in Rome, a climax of vital religious *aggiornamento* within my own Church. Among these decrees is an entire declaration expounding the duties and privileges of conscience, religious freedom, and moral dissent. The possibility of salvation is nuanced even to include non-theists, to the extent that they try to live out the imperatives of their own conscience. Catholics are encouraged to reject nothing that is true and holy in other world religious traditions. And the God behind all these faiths is described, not merely in personalist terms, but also as "ultimate and unutterable mystery," or "that hidden power which hovers over the course of things."

Most important, Vatican II condemns sheer undiscriminating obedience to civil law: "Actions which deliberately conflict with [universal natural law], as well as orders commanding such actions, are criminal. Blind obedience cannot excuse those who yield to them." And the conscientious objector is granted firm legitimacy: "It seems right that laws make humane provisions for the case of those who for reasons of conscience refuse to bear arms, provided however, that they accept some other form of service to the human community."[6]

The second key moment of 1965 was the unexpected Supreme Court Decision *U.S. versus Seeger,* which the New York Times once characterized as a short course in theology.[7] Since the Revolutionary War, the grounds for exempting conscientious objectors from military service had always been specific membership in the Quaker, Anabaptist, or some other pacifist sect. But during World War II cases had begun to emerge, based not on specific Church membership, but on a conscientious attitude against all war. In other words, many hoped to see conscience achieve rough parity with explicit religious guidelines like the Ten Commandments or other Church teachings.

Yet by 1958, congress in its amended Congressional Service Act had still restricted this conscientious objector exemption to cases "of religious training and belief." The wording at this point is murky. Religion here means only belief "in a relation to a Supreme Being involving duties superior to those arising from any human relation," but *not* including "essentially political, sociological, or philosophical views or a merely personal moral code." Congress clearly was seeking an umbrella broad enough to include the vagaries of more than two hundred sectarian creeds, but restrictive enough to exclude the draft boards' nightmare of a million unique cases.

Aware of interpretations like these, the Supreme Court's Seeger Decision of 1965 extended the basis for conscientious exemption by a quantum leap. Notice its functional criterion for picking out a valid religious alias: "Does the claimed belief occupy the same place in the life of the objector as an orthodox belief in God holds in the life of one clearly qualified for exemption?" Speaking for the court, Justice Tom Clark construed the notion of "Supreme Being" in the Selective Service Act broadly indeed. And as a corollary, he interpreted any exclusions beyond this scope as narrowly as possible. Congress had stated that "merely personal" values were not sufficient grounds. The court now reasoned that the phrase "merely personal" means a "moral code which is not only personal but which is the sole basis for the registrant's belief and is in no way related to a Supreme Being."

There is no doubt here that the court did its theological homework. As before, immunity for conscientious objectors could apply only to those who repudiate all war, not just this selected present war. But the range of religious legitimacy now widens to include the following situations: institutional or private faith, faith in one God or many, faith that chooses personal or impersonal models of the sacred. Moreover, the decision cites specific descriptions of the sacred—Hindu Brahman, Buddhist Nirvana, the "Hidden Power" mentioned in Vatican II, and theologian Paul Tillich's "power of Being, which works through those who have no name for it."

Observe how comprehensive the religious label here becomes. Deploring the inadequacy of human language to deal with ultimate questions, Justice Clark cautions local draft boards and courts that they cannot "reject beliefs because they consider them incomprehensible. Their task is to decide whether the beliefs professed by a registrant are sincerely held and whether they are, in the registrant's own scheme of things, religious."

Four years after the revolutionary Seeger Decision and Vatican II, I began volunteering as a draft counselor. I had just taught a course at the University of Detroit called "Dissent and Conscience in the American Experience," centering on the classical texts of civil disobedience. Students took up these ideas with passion, because they yearned for some plausible moral basis to refuse induction into a war that by now seemed immoral—and incidentally, futile. It was appalling how few citizens during those Vietnamese War years were acquainted with basic draft procedures, the recent Seeger Decision, or their own human rights. Deciding soon after this to join an active conscientious objector network in the wider Detroit area, I sought out registrants that might qualify for exemption.

For each case selected, I would interview the individual, offer help to complete a conscientious objector form and personal essay, and during later sessions, role-play in a tough Socratic coaching style to prepare candidates for their immanent local draft board defense. The most important hours were spent hearing out each value system, trying to grasp what touched a person most about happiness, love, work, the purpose of life. Some of these applicants belonged to readily labeled Christian pacifist Churches, but most had a deep religious world of their own, often dense and inarticulate. I was looking for any sense of ultimacy, a coherent ethic "in some way related to a Supreme Being," according to the court's minimal demand. I was tracking down the religious alias.

Superb illustrations of the values and hesitant affirmations I encountered daily are disclosed by Daniel Seeger, Arno Jakobson, and Forest Peter themselves, the three parties in *U.S. versus Seeger.* Their responses to the conscientious objector questionnaire show how cogent and yet inexpressible a private religious experience can be, especially when challenged to account for itself under fire. First question—do you believe in a Supreme Being? Forest Peter answers that it depends on definitions. "Human life for me is a final value . . . I suppose you could call that a belief in the Supreme Being or God. These just do not happen to be the words I use." Jakobson recognizes an ultimate cause or creator of all existence, which he terms "Godness," and the taking of human life a contradiction of that Godness inherent in other people.

To this same question, Seeger's response shows the most theological sophistication. "Of course, the existence of God cannot be proved or disproved," he says, "and the essence of his nature cannot be determined. I prefer to admit this and leave the question open rather than answer yes or no." But then he introduces a shrewd distinction.

Skepticism or disbelief in the existence of God does not necessarily mean lack of faith in anything whatsoever. For the martyrdom of Socrates shows that irony and skepticism may be consistent with positive faith. The Court of Appeals, in its earlier decision against Seeger, complaining of difficulties in pinning him down, conceded that perhaps there was almost no functional difference between Jakobson's devotion to a mystical force of "Godness" and Seeger's compulsion to "Goodness."

From Seeger's random affirmations, Justice Clark pieces together the rudiments of religious legitimacy, much in the way I would help registrants organize their own conscientious objector briefs. In summary, Clark thinks Seeger does in fact lay claim to a religious faith. Never overtly denying belief in a Supreme Being, Seeger holds that "the cosmic order does, perhaps, suggest a creative intelligence." Violence for him becomes a "spiritual crime." Most important, Seeger's behavior seems to confirm the sincerity of his words. Raised as a Catholic, recently a close student of the Quakers, he had been serving currently as a dedicated hospital orderly under the American Friends Service Committee. "We think it clear," says Clark, "that the beliefs which prompted Seeger's objection occupy the same place in his life as the belief in a traditional deity holds in the lives of his friends, the Quakers."

Were there any cowards or other counterfeits among the registrants I interviewed? Of course, I could never be certain. The arch-pacifist Gandhi himself used to insist that brave violence among his followers was morally preferable to cowardly nonviolence. Most of my applicants did seem "sincere," the minimal prerequisite which Justice Clark emphasized. Yet I was not surprised to find one warped feature recurring. A specific appeal to conscience might pass as religious in the minimal legal sense. However, its psychological foundations at times looked overly defensive and precarious, the more I heard about an applicant's family background. One man disdained violence, for instance, because of a vague pollyanna refusal to admit any brutality or negative feelings in himself or in others. He had been terrified by murderous impulses left exposed in his tantrums as a child. Or another applicant had determined to snuff out any legacy of his father's violence, whose raging binges used to threaten the whole family.

I could not discredit the present spirituality of these two registrants, of course—nor of any other human being—just because of its shaky origins. At any rate, the courts had never presumed to gauge psychological maturity in an individual conscientious objector. For every human being, it is essential to make allowances for what psychologist

Gordon Allport calls the functional autonomy of every religious drive. Perhaps most of us in childhood first chance upon some religious orientation as a distorted security measure, or then sustain it halfheartedly through adolescence as a shield of hollow conformity. What counts most is the mature way each individual lives out this faith as an adult.

For a while in my own life, I accustomed myself to reach out, anticipating prima facie resonance with fellow Catholics and other Christians, less by degrees with Jews, Muslims, Buddhists, and perhaps least with the stray agnostic or atheist. But experience itself has disrupted these tidy maps of intimacy. Today someone in the Peace Movement, Sanctuary, or Amnesty International, perhaps unchurched or agnostic, often shares deeper values with me than would, say, a fellow Catholic preoccupied about birth control or papal prerogatives. The religious alias does not just call expected loyalties into question. It also launches unpredictable new kinships.

Carl Jung once remarked that some of the best conversations and learning experiences of his life occurred with his schizophrenic patients. My own claim is modest, and far less incongruous. Through these religious conversations with so many conscientious objectors, my own spirituality drew inspiration and deepened. My range of empathy was stretched far beyond the cultural and spiritual boundaries that had once seemed impenetrable.

2

Sacred Inside, Sacred Outside

The previous chapter began by distinguishing an alias from a counterfeit. Then after sampling a spectrum of religious disguises, it attempted to differentiate the actual religious center from its many subtle dislocations.

As the legal basis for conscientious objection, a further difference emerged—between the official label of membership in a pacifist Church, and a more amorphous appeal to conscience or some private faith. The first sort of applicant appears socially and legally to belong. The other does not, and seems to drift in and out of legal recognition. Here are the religious insider and outsider—two differing styles of self-definition, and two ways of perceiving each other. The distinction is central to this chapter.

After describing these two unique spiritualities, and the barriers often leading to their misperception of each other, it will be easier to anticipate their characteristic preferences in prayer and other religious attitudes.

To Belong or Not to Belong

For courses in world religions at the University of San Francisco, I have long been assigning a major reflection paper on each student's individual faith position. Its purpose is twofold. Though many complete the semester with some informed respect for the faith of others, they might salvage just a patchwork of favorite insights, without trying to weave this wisdom into their own tradition, whatever it might be. Second, no sound comparison with anyone else's faith seems likely, except from a self-critical perspective adopted toward one's own.

Topics for the paper include first a delineation of each person's sacred center, whether friend or power or ultimate value; then the ideal attitudes and behavior expected of oneself and others; and finally, one's favorite solitary or corporate forms of worship and meditation. To clarify and tailor the project for each individual, there is a brief personal interview, based on a rough draft, before final writing.

As the two thousand or more interviews and papers have mounted through the past two decades, a few dominant patterns soon became evident. Though lacking a printout of statistics and sociological legerdemain, the ensuing distinction, rudimentary yet urgent, rests on plausible experience.

Two different handicaps keep recurring in student presentations, especially during their interviews. Let Jeanne represent the first complaint: "I belong to a specific religious tradition, which I myself joined or my family always professed. I understand and use its language. Yet I cannot find anything more unique than this to say about my individual spirituality." On the other hand, Coleen embodies the second complaint: "I do not at present belong to any specific religious tradition. Perhaps my family never did belong. Or my family belongs, but I am in process of rejecting this tradition. I lack any unique spirituality of my own."

Within the circle of identifiable religious communities, Jeanne fits almost too cozily as a religious insider. An official religious persona seems to take up most of her interior space. Beyond this circle she perceives outsiders like Coleen as directionless or maybe banished. It is premature to wager that Jeanne's own insider faith might be merely extrinsic—in developmentalist terms, a conventional rather than a post-conventional belief. On deeper scrutiny, such a faith could still prove genuinely personal, no matter how banal and sterile its presentation looks. Suggestions like the following might help Jeanne clarify her own position: Just mention the name Buddhist or Mormon or whatever your specific tradition, and list its tenets briefly, as you understand them. Explain to what extent you locate yourself at the margin or center of this official faith. Show what beliefs or values you now hold firmly or tentatively, and why. In other words, try to indicate the idiosyncratic ways you try to embody this shared public faith.

Though biased first to undervalue Jeanne's insider faith, an observer might be influenced conversely to romanticize Coleen's outsider faith. Her isolation looks so independent and savvy. But the faith beneath this mute confusion could prove shallow. Coleen needs more inclusive guidelines for writing than Jeanne does. If she lacks a so-called religious worldview, then she could try sketching her philosophy of life, or whatever she wants to call it. No need to play someone else's language game. And why waste time stating what she does not believe, or the ancestral creed no longer held? Beginning with her major values—attitudes toward this nation and environment, other persons, her own self—she gradually works her way toward any awareness of the sacred, or the closest equivalent to this factor in her experience. My encounter with Coleen, more so than with Jeanne, echoes step by step the many conscientious objector interviews mentioned in the previous chapter.

People like Jeanne and Coleen should be encouraged to view themselves exclusively as neither insider nor outsider, but as the combined insider-outsider. For an exaggerated emphasis on either polarity fosters religious complacency inside, or religious anomie outside the circle. On the other hand, we are each shaped by many forces beyond our control—circumstances of family and culture, religious indoctrination, individual temperament. To our advantage or misery, some of us are born or reborn within a perceived tradition, others not.

An Insider-Outsider Dialogue

As a close illustration of these two religious polarities, and also of their vital interaction, I want to reconstruct a religious discussion one afternoon about eight years ago with three Malaysian friends.

The conversation with Arthur and Achmad began at a San Francisco public swimming pool, continued at a nearby cafe, and ended in Achmad's small apartment, which he shared with his wife Sari, their young daughter, and another Malaysian family. Names and slight details will be disguised to guard confidentiality, but otherwise I can recount the exchange with accuracy. For it lasted six hours, an emotionally intense and exhilarating communication, which at the time stirred me so, that I outlined the discussion results right after returning home. I then mailed out three copies, asking each to confirm or modify my summary of their positions.

All were business undergraduate students from East Malaysia. Sari and Achmad were Malay Muslims in their mid-thirties, whereas Arthur, a Chinese in his mid-twenties, had no specified religious identity. I had taught Achmad and Sari a year before, and for months could scarcely glimpse the actual person entombed under Achmad's armor of Muslim orthodoxy. Both husband and wife kept prescribed daily hours of prayer and the rigors of their Ramadan fast with exactitude. But since Sari was less reticent about her own individual and family values, it was mostly through her mediation that I came to appreciate the human depth of both wife and husband.

Perhaps one reason for Achmad's remoteness was his insecurity at defending the Muslim tradition against a Catholic priest with unfair professorial advantage. He later mentioned wounds, too, from enforced recitation of Christian prayers in an Anglican grammar school, and from years of post-colonial resentment. Once the course in Asian religious traditions was finished, this couple had invited me for a few meals and parties, and soon we got to look forward to evenings together. By introducing me to their friend Arthur, the Hasan couple hoped I might have more empathy with Arthur's problems than they.

Arthur was an affable assertive person, honest to the point of cheek, as he himself admitted with laughter, in a quirky British accent. His East Malaysian background consisted of a Catholic grammar school and high school, but he could not yet fit into his local community where you were Christian, Muslim, Buddhist, Taoist, or a few other recognizable things. Otherwise you were nothing. He hated all religious sham, especially that of Muslim Malays back home. So it was miraculous that he and the Hasans, scrapping endlessly about Malaysian politics, could now turn into friends. They were three lonely expatriates huddling in a blizzard.

To me Arthur first introduced himself as a religious Nothing, in his own words. Achmad had often tried to convert him to Islam, and teams of smiling Mormons or apostles from the Church of the Open Door had pounded at his closed door, hounding him to get baptized. Though knowing how to confound most religious hucksters, he did confess anxiety about the odds against a Nothing getting to heaven. I took Arthur's concern in all seriousness, and as the Hasans listened quietly to us both, I tried to coax this "Nothing" label and detect an implicit religious "Something." Sari later dubbed this emerging religious alias the Arthurian heresy.

Arthur poured out more about his dreams, a passion for family honor, the tensions between spiritual integrity and a successful business career, plans for a just and humane Malaysian society, and a habit of praying each night to his faithful divine listener. Both Sari and Achmad were dumbfounded by their friend's well-buried religious secrets. After this, the four of us gradually assumed equal roles in an avid discussion, measuring the strength of newfound affinities. My post mortem outline later gives this summary of many unexpected agreements: all four of us believe in the same personal God and expect him to reward the morally good and punish the bad. It is sinful to murder, steal, or lie. We prefer talking to God in our own words. Each person must follow the claims of conscience. The best human life consists in unselfish service of others.

The Hasans and I felt a bond not shared by Arthur. As adults, we were now freely reaffirming the Muslim and Catholic traditions into which we had been born. Sensing that Arthur's view of life was far more optimistic than our own, we predicted he might find it tougher in time to sustain motivation as a generous activist, without support and fresh example from some spiritual community. Since the Hasans and I needed this group strength, and inspiration from our Sacred Scriptures, we wondered how Arthur could manage long without support like this.

On only two issues did Arthur and Achmad share a belief that differed from both Sari's and my own. They recognized experiences of black magic and a personal devil, whereas Sari and I tended to trace these middle-zone phenomena either to God above, or to the mysterious human unconscious within. These men yearned, too, to shield their women from the crude permissiveness of Western society, a caution Sari and I thought too demeaning and macho when we heard them work it out in detail. But at least Arthur and I agreed on the decisive topic that had initiated our long discussion. By following your conscience faithfully—with its demand for constant searching, hard scrutiny, openness to whatever God seems to ask—you can be saved.

To my regret, Achmad decided at the end of the evening, with sincere misgivings, that a loyal Muslim could only reject this overemphasis on conscience. As her husband explained himself, Sari kept an embarrassed silence, which I acknowledged politely, without challenge. For Achmad, an appeal to conscience sounded like slippery moral subjectivity. It might lead people to the precise sort of public laxity that he and Arthur had already deplored. He felt compassion for Arthur's inability to see further than conscience and a generic sort of God. Then Achmad admitted distress, too, at my own Jesus-idolatry, my indifference to the Qur'an's message of salvation. However, Sari had to remind him that Jews and Christians at least—maybe others, too—have a place of honor within Muslim tradition as People of the Book. After his wife's intervention, Achmad hesitated to speak confidently about damnation, either for Arthur or myself.

Achmad's last assertions cast a sobering proviso on the evening. Yet Sari, Arthur, and I were touched by his reluctance and sadness, which undercut any sure censure against his friends. Perhaps more deeply than Achmad himself, Arthur and I could sense the uneasy truce between Achmad's private religious sensitivity and his interpretation of the public Muslim tradition. At the evening's end, I reminded the Hasans I could not accept the Muslim faith for myself, but respected both of them for adhering to their own tradition. I thought all four of us would be judged by God on the fidelity with which each of us followed our conscience—Arthur in his Arthurian way, Achmad and Sari in their Muslim way, and I in my Christian way.

Two years after this conversation, on a research trip to Nepal, I stopped for three weeks with Arthur, the Hasans, and their extended families in East Malaysia. There I had a better chance to observe the hospitality, everyday customs, political conflicts, and religious influences all three had often reported. I was asked to divide my time between two worlds, each with its own strongly partisan claims, Chinese and Malay, now an afternoon with Arthur, now an evening with Achmad and Sari. The Arthur-Hasan kinship, assured during one six-hour discussion in San Francisco, now showed strain in handling congealed local grievances. We spent hours at separate offices where each man worked, at their homes, places of worship, forays to beaches and jungles. I met their various relatives and friends, and even a few of their former teachers.

The Hasan family were eager, as expected, to set up a meeting with the Mufti leader of their community. Through translators, the elderly man asked me within moments after our introduction, why I thought so many local Christians were converting to Islam. Without waiting for an answer, he then wondered how soon I intended to become a Muslim myself. In response, my words dropped like ponderous aphorisms in translation, phrase by phrase. I suggested we both pray that he become a better Muslim and I a better Christian. A polite ecumenical cliché, I know. Though smiling in agreement, the Mufti admitted it had seldom been his custom to pray that way.

Reflecting back on the earlier conversation in San Francisco, I am convinced a gestalt shift is mostly what a religious outsider like Arthur really needs. Arthur must perceive himself, not outside or at the margins of someone else's circle of coherence, but at the center of his own circle. By lending him a few insights and words at the precise moment he reaches for them, I felt the delight of a Socratic midwife, offering the appropriate catalyst for insight. Like people surprised to learn they have been speaking prose all their lives, religious outsiders are reminded that they, too, have perhaps long been religious. For individual religious identity must not depend on someone else's arbitrary maps of our common religious turf.

An insider like Achmad, on the other hand, needs a better appreciation of Arthur's religious alias, and also of likely counterfeits within a Muslim's own circle of coherence. It has been observed that the best doctors never forget the potential patient in themselves, teachers the potential student, priests the potential sinner. In discussion with Arthur and myself, perhaps the Hasans' finest moment was an honest bafflement at Arthur's confession to so many values and experiences they had to call religious. In this recognition scene, both husband and wife felt religious identity with the outsider. Yet Achmad at last could only view Arthur as a potential Muslim—or rather, a potential Achmad, not yet a unique Arthur.

Another crucial moment occurred for Sari, especially. The Hasans felt the dissonance between a warm individual kinship with both their guests and what Achmad remembered of conventional Muslim cautions against dangers in such friendship. Perhaps spiritual maturity is impossible unless the insider first learns to live with tensions like these: the paradoxes of faith-doubt, public-private faith, outsider saint-insider sinner, the fallible interpretations of infallible truth.

Common Prayer: The Insider Way

As part of their insider worldview, people like Sari and Achmad also show distinctive patterns of meditation or prayer. Common Prayer seems a suitable name to describe this particular path, with its overtones of a coherent heritage preexisting and shaping the individual person. It can be exemplified most readily in religious traditions of the West, with their scriptural and prophetic emphasis, distinct institutions, and express criteria for membership. In a later section of this chapter, Prayer Incognito will connote the random, improvisational path of outsiders like Arthur.

Throughout this study, prayer means any personal, impersonal, or transpersonal way to express communion with the sacred. In the student essays mentioned before, one assigned area deals with each person's unique prayer experiences or worship. What has emerged in their responses is an incredible breadth of spiritually expressive behavior: rites and sacraments, fixed and casual prayer forms, meditation, yoga or athletic routines, openness to natural beauty, deep reflection on one's conscience, tradeoffs with luck or taboos or preternatural forces. As illustrations for the Common and Incognito patterns in later pages, I shall draw upon various sources, including contemporary fiction and autobiography, my own counseling experiences, but notably these student accounts.

Abdul-Aziz, a close friend of the Hasan couple, attends their same local mosque. For me, this young Yemenese Muslim seems to personify the better features of Common Prayer. He has long immersed himself in a resonant spiritual heritage. Ever since his earliest years, he would engage in *salat* formal prayers five times daily, and frequent *dua* or informal conversation with God. My few visits with him and his sister were spent listening to his expressive readings from favorite Arab poets and the Qur'an, with indispensable translations. "My grandmother always used to encourage me to read some of the Qur'an each night before going to sleep," he once told me. "That way, I would dream of the angels. I believe she was right, for I still dream of them." Throughout childhood he committed almost the entire Qur'an to memory, feeling it in the marrow, and by now he is only beginning to understand it.

Abdul meditates, too, in the sense of resting quietly in God's presence. But his primary sense of prayer is reciting and pondering the sacred text, engaging in it body and mind, letting it penetrate his imagination. "Whenever I read the words," he says, "I feel I am watching the lips of Allah, and hearing him speak these words to me." This praying style is a genuine faith searching for insight—*fides quaerens intellectum.* For the sacred mystery must first be experienced and lived before it can be fathomed. Trying to understand it can only be gradual, but a process ever incomplete. Abdul is trying to shape a unique Muslim imagination, to stock it with images and phrases from the Qur'an, the same way many devout Jews or Christians pray over the Torah and Gospel.

A partiality toward formal Muslim prayer or any other fixed textual tradition often springs from a distrust of individual self-indulgence. This familiar counterfeit implies wallowing in one's own stale religious obsessions. Sermons or public liturgies impose this solipsistic experience on a captive audience. Weary of such public displays, and also the catchwords and dull TV patter often packaged as spontaneous group prayer, many people have turned back to reexamine the old devotions and formulas in their own heritage. This return to sources recalls the caution by theologian Karl Rahner not to discard dogmas that seem mere empty baggage today. They should be permitted to recede back into the believing Unconscious of one's tradition, and handled gently like distant relatives. For they might take on surprising importance tomorrow.

The rosary and monastic Divine Office, for instance, abandoned three decades ago as ritualistic chatter, have been rediscovered by some Catholics today. In his prison meditations, too, Dietrich Bonhoeffer often found new wisdom in the overfamiliar lines of some Lutheran hymn, the early conciliar creeds, or the catechism. Prayer forms like these can function as a secure disciplined setting, a sort of background music releasing the mind from its own busy-work. In our present era of excessive subjectivity, the very recalcitrance and objectivity of a prayer heritage can be experienced as a metaphor for God's transcendent otherness. Coming from outside and beyond you, this presence may shock and rub raw, confronting you with ideas and images that your mind is not yet prepared to handle. In meditating on the text, you ponder and yield, trying to measure up to its demands.[1]

Unless this heritage is assimilated thoroughly into your own bloodstream, how can you venture to speak as a theologian, trying to represent your own official tradition, shared by so many others? A Jesuit theologian colleague of mine prepares his sermons by meditating each morning on a different biblical passage, the text assigned for that day's liturgy. Reading it several times slowly, he is alert for any phrase that stirs or gives voice to his deepest yearnings. And beginning to chant this phrase as a mantra, he listens closely to it, trying to let it become the root of silent prayer throughout that day.

This illustration introduces a blend of classical prayer traditions from East and West. A text from the Vedas, Lotus Sutra, Qur'an, or Bible, and then its slow, nuanced incorporation into the individual psyche. One of my Chinese students from Singapore meditates this way on Taoist scriptures, especially the I Ching. Modifying the conventional rites of divination, she tosses the yarrow stalks or coins each morning to discover an assigned Hexagram. This then becomes her text and mantra source for that day of prayer. Most important, she tries to respect this mantra as a gift from beyond herself, not just the result of her own compulsions.

Prayer for Its Own Sake

Like anything else, focus on the unyielding text or prayer tradition can be pushed to extremity. Two exaggerations will now be singled out for comment—literalness first, and then conformity that has become an end in itself.

Exemplifying the first extreme, some students admit resorting to their Bible as a pious lottery or horoscope. A passage surfacing at random will determine which target to phone for a date, which dress to wear for an auspicious job interview. With scarcely more sophistication than this, many fundamentalists treat their entire Qur'an or Bible uncritically as a compendium of all knowledge. Christian Creationists among my students, for instance, write about marvelous parallels between various geological theories and remote biblical passages, often literally interpreted. One Muslim stretches a few isolated Qur'an images or verses into God's miraculous anticipations of modern embryology and astro-physics, not to mention utopian tax laws and penal codes.

Against a campaign by some intrusive critics to demystify the sacred text, it makes sense that the fundamentalist is tempted to counter with a self-protective literalness. Yet in one sense, this fierce devotion to the text is itself an implied idolatry. It mistakes the shadows for reality, as psychologist Norman Brown observes, "taking unconscious projections of the human spirit as autonomous powers; letting the metaphors go dead, and then, when dead, bowing down before them, taking them literally."[2]

Thus, to guard its integrity, I think each fixed textual tradition needs to reach beyond itself. My own Catholic legacy has taught me the importance of recognizing the same God of the Bible or Qur'an speaking also through other voices. This includes my own personal spiritual experience, religious traditions other than my own, the classics of literature and art, knowledge from all the human sciences, each with its own relatively autonomous methods. Moreover, a fervent receptivity toward the tradition and text must not stand alone without its balancing corrective. At prayer, for instance, liturgist Mary Collins tends to repeat a biblical passage slowly, savoring the words to discover their paradox and challenge. Because the day's activities interfere, such distractions can be handled as a welcome counterpoint. As both sources interweave and compete, her meditation does not simply attend to God's Word, but wrestles with it. Like Jeremiah, Job, and the Psalmists, she prays even by arguing and proposing alternatives.[3]

The second excess introduced above, conformity simply for the sake of conformity, or Common Prayer *ex opere operato,* is more difficult to pin down. At times you admire the wistful clinging to a sacred heritage, even when its prayer forms are scarcely understood. One of the most famous Hasidic tales describes a gradual distancing of successive generations from their central religious rituals. A rabbi of the first generation would carry his people's burden to God by lighting a fire and saying a prayer at a definite place in the woods. In this final era, after the erosion of successive ritual details through history, a rabbi sits in his chair and realizes he does not know the prayer, the spot in the woods, nor how to light the fire. But at least he can tell the story about how it was once accomplished.

Yet in his short story "The Blessing," on the other hand, Hugh Nissenson's main character understands himself precisely as someone who cannot perform blind rituals like those of the Hasidic rabbi. Stunned by news of his eight-year-old son's death from cancer, Yitshaak refuses to say the conventional "Blessed art Thou, O Lord," prayer at the approaching funeral rites. For it would seem monstrous and humiliating to sanctify God's apparent crime. However, his Aunt

Esther, whose own faith had been tested in the Belsen concentration camp long ago, presses him to say the words anyway, even if the familiar Hebrew god-image and verses seem to collide against his immediate grief and anger.[4]

Often in counseling sessions, especially during hospital chaplaincy, I have listened to people in disruptive conditions like these. Unable or unwilling to lean back on their Common Prayer formulas, they do not expect suitable religious attitudes to catch up eventually with a wooden recitation now. For such an effort smacks of hypocrisy, and many people want their words to match only what they sincerely feel. At the end of Nissenson's story, Esther on their home balcony proceeds with evening prayers, as expected, addressed to the orderly stars. For she has never ceased blessing God her tormentor. But Yitshaak, rebelling against the orderly formulas and sky, feels ''excluded by the tumult of his heart.'' He seems banished from Esther's prayer tradition, with no perception that his tears themselves, and the very wrestling with God, might be his one truly relevant prayer.

Prayer Incognito: The Outsider Way

As stated before, outsiders often perceive their own prayer as nonexistent, incoherent, or at least falling short of the insider touchstone. What they themselves perceive as rebellious or novel in their own experience, however, is usually a religious commonplace within an extant, viable tradition somewhere else. For example, what seems new about New Age Spirituality in the United States is actually very old—the traditional rites and prayer forms of Buddhists, Hindus, or Primal peoples, now reinterpreted in a new context.

Thus, it is useless to sweep all this rich spiritual improvisation under the single outsider label, unless you recognize how close or distant it gauges itself to someone else's shared heritage. The *incognito* term here will embrace an outsider's various uncharted ways of communing with the sacred. Also the term suggests a broad spread of free verse forms for those insiders wishing to abandon or supplement their fixed textual heritage, as they perceive it.

Yet an immediate question arises. The Common Prayer tradition in most world spiritualities, if properly interpreted, is already wide enough to embrace most impromptu prayer forms. Even the Abrahamic family of religions have their Hasidic, Christian, and Sufi heritage of mysticism. So why should anyone encourage exclusion first, or second, the need to drift outside the circle, merely to pray in one's own way? One answer was offered in the preceding section, an excessive literalness and conformity. Once the group itself yields to such attitudes, individual members with a more legalistic temperament can be expected to constrict the norms for belonging.

In the Nissenson tale just recounted, Yitshaak feels harsh disparity between his own heart and the aloof objectivity of inherited prayer formulas, which his aunt imposes on him. Yet if the tragic Job and many of Yitshaak's own ancestors could stand alongside him, protesting from inside the textual tradition, their prayer might sound more like the following: "Unfairness in the Bible used to upset me," writes one of my students, describing herself as a contented outsider. "Jacob having to work so long to get Rachel, Isaac playing favorites with Jacob, and Jacob doing the same with Joseph. Toward God I often feel like a rebellious child, arguing with my father. I feel at times he is somewhat disappointed, but generally trusting. I'm given a long leash and can roam freely, but occasionally he jerks the leash to let me know who is in control. Sometimes I get annoyed with his interference in my life, and don't know what he is up to. I tell him I don't need what he is trying to teach me, and that my life is none of his business."

A second, more specific reason for this disparity between the public tradition and an individual's unique spirituality can be traced to the unconscious bias in some spiritual directors. Adopting a few privileged types of meditation patterned closely after the Common Prayer model, such people are prone to demean or dismiss alternatives. While searching for my own compatible forms of prayer, I have clashed sometimes with gurus of this type.

Two of these experiences I think representative enough to deserve retelling. Once near Bangkok, attending the daily audience given by a famous Buddhist abbot, I was suddenly singled out from the crowd, no doubt as the one obvious Christian foreigner present. "Do you meditate?" the monk addressed me through his translators. After getting him to define the term, I said, "Yes." But he smiled, and added, "Give me two weeks with you, and I'll teach you really how to meditate!" After this exchange recurred a few more times, I realized his translators had not erred. The monk just presumed that Vipassana, a form of intense imageless meditation favored by his own Theravada tradition, must lie beyond an uninitiated grasp, and that my own form of meditation had to be inferior. Though doubtful that anything so far beyond my unaided skill could now be inculcated in just two weeks, I was still ready to waive his apparent condescension or smugness and try out the Buddhist method.

Years before this Thailand experience, I began spiritual formation as a Jesuit, guided by well-intentioned elders, who presumed, again, the nonexistence or inferiority of any earlier spirituality of my own. For the next ten years, I would spend a delightful quarter hour each evening before bedtime writing in my journal, gazing at the sunset, and casually anticipating highlights of the discursive meditation hour at dawn. But the formal hour itself, next morning or any other time of day, often became a tedious combat with distractions. I could skip this formal hour for a week and feel only a broken obligation. Yet a week of omitted evening preparations left me feeling incomplete and scattered. My private Copernican revolution consisted eventually in expanding the evening methods and endorsing them as my own distinctive prayer.

On one occasion, after explaining this alternative style of meditation to an elderly Jesuit spiritual guide, I drew a disappointing response: "Deep feelings and ruminations, yes. But don't call them prayer or meditation!" The man heard out my emphasis on prayerfulness rather than measurable acts of prayer; on communion with now the personal Christian God, now the transpersonal God of the biblical Wisdom tradition. He admitted fears that I might compromise or discredit the only disciplined prayer routine he trusted.

Range of Breaking Free

To clarify the overwhelming diversity of prayer forms open to the free spirit, you can first distinguish those individuals still in process of cutting loose from Common Prayer conventions. Gradually the spectrum shades off toward those perceiving themselves with little or no relationship to any specific religious tradition.

A remarkable portrayal of the transition from an unquestioned Common Prayer background to a unique outsider spirituality occurs in Gayle Baney Whittier's story, "Lost Time Accident."[5] A sensitive girl, apparently in her pre-teens, determines to pray as never before for the recovery of a family friend, injured seriously in an industrial accident. As preparation for her fixed textual rituals, Anne first dusts and straightens her room, then takes out a white prayerbook to find the correct prayer. The first impulse is to promise God she will read her Bible more often, but Anne dislikes this hint of bribery. The Renaissance cadences in these set prayers from the book make her stumble, so she begins wondering if a spontaneous prayer, using words of her own century, would not be better. But how is God to be addressed? "Heavenly" feels too distant, "Father" too close, "God Almighty" too familiar a curse between her father and mother.

All the names of God begin to sound unctuous and strange, echoing the cadences of the family's local preacher. At this groping stage,

Anne settles upon a direct plea, "God, please help Stash." But then, adding the phrase, "in your infinite mercy," she recognizes its bookish, derivative quality, as if miracles must be performed just to vindicate these self-serving words. Suddenly a great space opens up, "between the outgrown child who had dared to pray, and this self-conscious stranger who suddenly could not." After a long silence, her imagination drifts slowly toward the distant hospital and hovers near the dying man. Her dreaming hands begin to circle over the body, and press gently against veins and skin, her will contracting into a force meant to summon back his life. With the gestures of a healer, Anne concludes: "Breathing for us both, for myself and for the dying man, . . . among my vanquished gods, I began my work in the world."

This same wariness against reverting to God's traditional names can be found in the comedian George Carlin's efforts to free himself from the confinements of his own Irish Catholic tradition. From the age of six to twelve, he would go into a church to talk alone with God: "Well, God, I'm not gonna leave now until someone else comes in." But later as an adult, he substitutes for "God" the phrase "Pleasegod," which to him implies "Please, Universe," a larger sacred cosmos of which Carlin is only a part. At present a mature man standing before God, he wants to avoid cowering for favors. The name he has created for God is "Dwen," an attempt to sidestep the psychological and historical garbage associated with all God's standard names.[6]

Most of the acknowledged outsiders among my students write about casual dialogue with God, viewed as a friend, interlocutor, or readily available guide. Yet some consciously push away from this conventional direct relationship, and make an important distinction. "I rarely pray in the strict sense," one writer specifies. "At times I may address a question to no one in particular, but to someone or something like God. Why am I here, or why me? In reflective moods I begin talking with myself, as if someone present were sharing my conversation or overhearing it."

Often these student compositions describe free-floating meditation during mountain and forest treks, or on skis and surfboards, a spiritual experience familiar to many of us. Charles Sanders Peirce, the founder of American Pragmatism, calls this process *musement*, which means spiritual reverie, pure play, contemplative recreation, with no rules. "There's nothing else like fishing in Alaska," one student writes. "It's a feeling of total calm and purity that encompasses everything and sets me at peace with myself. I call it a spiritual experience because I don't view myself as religious." At home, behind his drum set, he feels in a sort of temple. "I tune everything out that is not part of the music, and set an invisible boundary between myself and the rest of the world. Then my music opens me up to God. It's my secret communion, a covenant with God that only I know about.''

A young nurse, too, explains her efforts to find just the right setting and attitudes for her own Taoist experience. She prays best near the sea or mountains, where an individual feels dwarfed by superior powers. ''I've always found it difficult to pray or worship in a so-called house of God. I don't like images of God around. I would rather experience the world's beauty and heartache as the force of God.'' A corner of her dormitory room once held a kneeling pad, leaves, fresh flowers, assorted gems, and incense to be burned during meditation. ''It took me many months until I felt my personal energy in this corner had been established. I found it unnerving when a friend would get curious and touch the objects in my corner or kneel down in my space.'' Gradually able to separate these sacred props from the religious center within herself, she found out how to ''transcend without them into another space and time.''

With almost no boundaries to this variegated range of prayer forms, perhaps the test-case would be the prayer of an explicit atheist. It is crucial, of course, to be alert for traces of any religious alias in this person's experience. At times the nominal atheist, implicitly adhering to an impersonal model of the sacred, is only rejecting some specific personal god-image, such as the old bearded puppeteer or busy-body judge. Again, an atheist may be communing with conscience or the cosmos, much in the way some explicit theists meditate on the abstract Dharma or Tao. Neo-Marxists Roger Garaudy and Ernst Bloch, for instance, interpret the conventional god-image as a projected hope for humanity's long awaited future, a cry for the Absolute. This hope itself is a symbol worthy of contemplation and religious awe. What strikes the imagination as an absent God is in fact our humanity itself in the process of being born.

The ex-seminarian Kallistratov in Chingiz Aitmatov's novel *The Place of the Skull* introduces the anomalous god-image just described, which he calls the ''God of Tomorrow,'' with no existence independent of our awareness. In a letter to his fiancee, he mentions his awestruck response to a recent Bulgarian choral concert. The anthems of this church choir derive from centuries of human creativity, ''to keep alive him whom they had invented to symbolize the spiritual heights for which man reaches out instinctively.'' The liturgical texts addressed to God are just a pretext for celebrating the courageous human spirit. Communion with and celebration of this ''human spirit,'' then, is Kallistratov's distinctive form of prayer. His god-image could be described as a "shadowy world that consists of all dreams, memories, longings, pangs of remorse, all the joys and sorrows, gains and losses that make up the individual's path through life."[7] Transposed into Marx's classical formulation, here is the heart of a heartless world.

To the traditional theist, Kallistratov's view of prayer is certainly heterodox, and indeed the Russian Orthodox seminary rector in this novel expels the young man for maintaining it. Yet Kallistratov's outsider prayer blends readily into the insider legacy of Hindu Vedantists and other cosmic pantheists. And it also approximates the faith of someone like Jung, who recognizes no objective God separate from the mind's archetypal god-image.

In this analysis of individuals placing themselves religiously inside or outside, it is wise to recall once more that the religious center, as defined in the previous chapter, actually underlies both inside and outside. Moreover, most insider traditions, if interpreted generously, will stretch wide enough to include almost any extempore prayer form. However, the perception of belonging or not belonging must be acknowledged as a crucial psychological and cultural factor. In a similar way, the fact that separate religious traditions exist should never be minimized as a concrete historical reality.

Because the two distinctive prayer situations described in this chapter do overlap readily, both could be experienced together at once or in sequence. As remarked before, the ideal is to view oneself dialectically as the combined religious insider-outsider.

3

An Imagination of the Sacred

The sacred, as thus far described, is both too massive and too fragile for the finite human mind. But this mystery is rendered even more inaccessible to imaginations handicapped by their very culture or temperament. Chapter 1 found some spiritual experiences that had been rendered unrecognizable by a filter of language and unquestioned legal or social assumptions. And chapter 2 traced how an experience of not belonging can impair religious self-definition.

Yet these are just a few of many factors shaping each person's unique perception of the sacred. As an illustration, you might take a comprehensive glance at your own talents and quirks of personality. With some difficulty, you can sift out those attributes common to all people, those shared only with some other people, and those unique to yourself. These are respectively the universal, the cultural, and the individual dimensions of any experience.

This threefold distinction, too, may clarify the complex dimensions of your religious self-understanding. First, as a basic human being, you are a homo religiosus, in the language of Mircea Eliade. All of us are engaged on a spiritual journey evoked by metaphors of flight, combat, spiritual courtship, homecoming, or rebirth—symbols spun from the finite imagination belonging to everyone. Second, as an individual rooted in a specific history, however, you share particular spiritual kinship, in various overlapping circles, with anyone of your temperament and characteristic spirituality, your gender, race, culture, era, and religious tradition. And third, you have your own unique experience of the sacred, an idiosyncratic god-image, or as Mahatma Gandhi always insisted, an individual religion.

With these terms understood, it is time to state a simple governing principle. No religious symbol or attitude, especially the alias and counterfeit, can be interpreted accurately without scrutiny of all three dimensions—universal, cultural, and individual. This principle has special impact on two interactions: the first between a public religious heritage and your own private religious experience, and the second between your unique god-image and unique self-image.

This chapter first develops the latter dialectic between your own god-image and self-image, without slighting the effects of culture and religious heritage. Then it explores some widespread and often misunderstood sacred aliases—ghosts, saints, magic, and finally, their eerie underside, the satanic and daimonic.

Self-Image and Sacred Image

Imagine two individuals, both socialized to the same extent within one shared culture and religious tradition. Then try to account for their individual religious differences by a few measurable factors. These components would include their own free preferences, their separate developmental history, specific projections drawn from parents and other major role models, but especially each person's unique self-image.

Today most people recognize how thoroughly any individual's experience of self-worth permeates an entire perceptual world, not just an attitude toward the sacred. For example, in one visualization exercise, young children first relaxed and imagined a guided fantasy, then tried to draw it, and finally, gave an oral interpretation of their crayon picture to a psychologist. They were asked to view themselves as rose bushes, noting careful details about flowers, branches, and setting. "What do you look like? Tell me about your flowers, your leaves and roots. Who takes care of you?"

Children who were popular with their teacher and playmates drew themselves as blooming roses, with prominent sun, birds, shrubbery. Some with an alleged history of sexual abuse surrounded their roses with protective fences, large thorns, barred doorways, with commentaries like these: "A woodsman came and tried to cut me down, but I wouldn't let him." Or "Look at all the caterpillar eggs on the leaves," or "A bee came along to take some stuff out of it, but the rose didn't want to be touched."[1]

You would expect the two groups to carry with them this same differing filter of perceptions and feelings as they approached the sacred. Thus, in another psychological survey, adults with a nurturing God commonly viewed themselves as generous and forgiving. Those with a strict disciplinary God distrusted the motives of other people. Another type of questionnaire poses this topic: "There are many different ways of picturing God. On a scale of 1-7, where would you place yourself between the two contrasting images in each set—

mother and father, master and spouse, judge and lover, friend and king, creator and healer, redeemer and liberator?" Despite contrary predictions, the responses to this survey showed no direct correlation with age, sex, education, or church attendance. However, those midway in the scale tended to hold more liberal attitudes toward minorities, the death penalty, and presidential candidates.

A more elusive factor behind an individual's preferred image is suggested by Rorschach test interpretations. In a typical "vista" response to one specific ink-blot image, you might associate that figure with a stairway or a bridge between mountains. If this pattern recurs in interpreting other samples, you seem to betray a heightened sense of distance and separateness in handling space. The analyst might conjecture, then, that you tend to locate authority outside the self, and chafe under a tyrannical superego. You probably worship a God distant and powerful, a transcendent law-giver that must be broached across a hazardous mythical space for forgiveness.[2]

Such analyses as these are useful, but too many psychologists take one crucial component for granted. Focusing on an individual choice, they may underestimate how a specific religious heritage itself can sway someone away from any human image, or toward some favored image, such as the remote disciplinary God. Most religious traditions make allowance for two distinctive uses of the imagination. First is the kataphatic way, the way of affirmation, offering intimacy with a personal god or gods. Some traditions encourage, others forbid, the representation of this personal factor by human images. Second is the apophatic way of negation, the Via Negativa. Abandoning human love and any human facsimile, it seeks communion with the Absolute, a source beyond all personal or even impersonal attributes. Both ways have their own distinctive logic and grammar. Sin in the kataphatic, for instance, tends to be an alien love that disrupts the love relationship with a personal God. In the apophatic it tends to be any ignorance that clouds an unfolding spiritual enlightenment and liberation.

Whereas the Hindu, Tantric Buddhist, and Primal traditions present all these options to the individual, other traditions may exclude or neglect one of the above ways. For example, the Taoist or Zen Buddhist apophatic legacy purifies the mind of inferior comparisons, and this newfound emptiness itself becomes a symbol of transcendent completeness. Or the Muslim and Jewish religious style, kataphatic but stripped of pictures and statues, might look visually barren at first, until you grasp its advantages. For the creative imagination is funneled toward just a few vital symbols—a book and its calligraphy, particular sacred places, people, historical moments, rituals of solidarity. And left unspoiled by the clichés of Renaissance and St. Sulpice artists, each individual imagination is prodded to add its unique touches.

The previous chapter probed into some resourceful ways an individual might repudiate, quarrel, or compromise with a Common Prayer tradition. For anyone retaining identity within the religious group, there is usually some trade-off between the official religious heritage and an individual's private spirituality. Mark Twain catches a few of these lopsided compromises by an effective parody. Christians pray publicly at church for a heaven. Yet this is a realm idealized far differently from actual values in their private moral and aesthetic life—singing, harp-plucking, celibacy, interracial intimacy, and endless hosannas to a God basking in vain flattery. Also, the Recording Angel has to cancel public invocations for good weather, clothing and shelter for the destitute, or forgiveness of enemies. For in private the individual wants business rivals struck down with deafness, more threatening weather so that coal prices double, and a cheaper, more exploitable work force. In other words, official Church rhetoric often contradicts secret wishes of the heart.[3]

Our imaginations have been influenced, at times manipulated, by the religious images that others left behind them. Raphael's madonnas, Michelangelo's creator, or El Greco's suffering Christ succeed so well that some people can no longer imagine anything different.

Yet in Yogjakarta, Indonesia, I once visited a Catholic chapel with about fifty original paintings of various Old and New Testament scenes, a stunning gallery that I felt compelled to preserve on slides. The priest had commissioned a handful of amateur artists in a Balinese village totally Hindu in population, touched by little or no contact with Christian iconography. For each picture, he would first read them a biblical passage, discuss it with the artists in an allegedly non-directive way, and then urge them to paint it according to their own unique interpretation. Though a few canvases just substituted Hindu poster clichés for predictable Christian ones, most of the art freed visitors from the United States or Europe for a fresh re-imagining.

The Religious Middle Zone

In their essays and interviews many of my international students do not speak of a god-image at all. Instead they represent the sacred by ancestors, or diffusive spiritual forces for good and evil. Prayer and healing occur only in this dramatic setting. What the historian Tetsuo Yamaori observes about Shinto and other Japanese folk traditions can apply to many other cultures as well. He compares the role of ancestral spirits in Japan to the authority and function of the Judeo-Christian God in Eurocentric societies. No physical or mental suffering will be cured until the ancestors are remembered daily and treated with more respect. This attitude prevails even among Buddhists, whose theology would otherwise stress reincarnation. Famous people in Japanese history often become local tutelary *kami,* with their own distinctive shrines and festivals.[4]

Though I used to discount the anxiety of my clients about sorcery or hungry ghosts, I am now learning daily a cross-cultural counselor's respect for the polychrome spectrum of religious aliases. This realm of the preternatural is truly a middle zone.[5] Since the eighteenth century, science and philosophy in the West have influenced our imagination of a two-tiered cosmos. There is first the natural domain, based on experimental observation. Second is the supernatural domain, based on sacred revelation. The first tier includes human beings and natural forces; the second, God and spiritual cosmic forces. However, between these two realms, many folk cultures throughout East and West add a third—a broad middle realm including ancestral and local nature spirits, ghosts and demons, astrological forces, curses, the evil eye, the power of charms and amulets and other magic.

If a landslide kills three people, for example, many of us would attribute this tragedy to the natural laws of probability from the first tier, or possibly to God's providence or direct intervention from the second. However, someone belonging to a culture with a rich middle zone will not be satisfied with unintelligible chance, but demand: "Why were these three specific people in this spot at this particular time?" And since such a calamity is hard for any believer to attribute directly to a loving God, it is associated instead with witchcraft, demons, hungry ghosts, or astrology.

The Sacred Dead

A convincing introduction to middle-zone experiences is to overhear the implicit dialogue many people have with their dead. "The only place in the natural outdoors where I as a child ever encountered God," a French Catholic student writes, "was at my grandfather's grave, located in a small rural church cemetery. I talked to him in my prayers, making sure he was okay, and asking him to watch over me. I was convinced God would assign him the task of my guardian angel." A young Presbyterian, too, whose father died ten years before, now pays tribute to their continuing spiritual relationship. He can still visualize his father sprawled in the driver's seat, smoking a cigar, advising the nine-year-old how to repair his minibike. "Prayer often means conversations with my dad, who today still stands for authority, direction, and hope. I tell him my difficulties, and try to think how he would solve them in his own way. He had a knack for handling problems with the utmost confidence and interest, like a scientist making a great discovery. This spiritual process of mine keeps me close to my dad, and helps me remember how he looked and acted.''

Traditional societies that pay extraordinary respect to their live elders, especially in Africa, China, and most of Asia, show consistency in seeking the mediation and advice of these lordly presences after death. So many prayer experiences and family rituals of my Chinese students, for example, center on their relationship with the entire clan, many of whom now reach back from the spirit world to make contact with living relatives. At least once a year, some of the more affluent traditional Chinese families converge from great distances to celebrate a gravesite reunion in Hong Kong or Taiwan, trying to maintain a stable emotional and religious bond with the dead. In fact, many Taoist temples I have visited in Hawaii, Hong Kong, and Taiwan are lined wall after wall with snapshots of the recent dead.

The Christian counterpart to this active middle zone can be found at shrines to the Virgin Mary or a local patron saint, still prominent in many rural Catholic communities, notably those of Latin countries. Commonly invoked by diminutives, like nicknames given to villagers, the statue itself is treated as most renowned member of the community, and given a privileged spot in processions or civil inaugurals. Often separated geographically from the parish church, priest, and sacraments, the shrine is last sanctuary even for those distant from other religious institutions. Though church buildings and their statues were devastated during the Spanish Civil War, for example, shrine images were usually spared, because they seemed identified with the pain and needs of every commoner, no matter what ideology. Trusting their saint to put in a good word for them, villagers count on a sympathetic hearing at the shrine. After all, the sacred figure is a longstanding village member, and no one else is so knowledgeable about the local weather and politics.[6]

It seems ironic that while still alive, the saints cherished ideals almost antagonistic to the values for which many of their devotees now prize them. Once a hero or heroine renouncing worldly possessions, now the saint is approached often as just a wonder-worker, a pipeline of materialistic favors. This anomaly is illustrated pointedly in the lives of devout Buddhist monks, Hindu yogis, and the early Christian desert ascetics. The most austere and otherworldly is prized as a source of grace in which lay devotees hope to share. Admired for renunciation, the saintly figure is hounded away to retreats successively more remote, in order to escape the temptation of further gifts and adulation.

One distinct feature about middle-zone experience is its fascination with the exact spell or ritual, an undeniable seed-bed for obsessive personalities. I have even met people searching for the conclusive prayer formula that God could not possibly turn down. Some traditional mantras, a chain-letter novena, or a series of attended Masses, if prayed in the right disposition, do indeed promise a happy death, or the grace of final repentance. The Hindu upanyana sacred thread, the Catholic scapular medal of the Virgin, a Buddhist consecrated strip of cloth with the Kuan Yin image—these will allegedly protect the devotee's body, as long as the amulet is worn.

In my own childhood, our loss of a school football game would often elicit this reproof from one elderly nun: "I know you prayed, boys and girls, but did you pray to St. Anthony?" Luther and Erasmus had great fun over these specialized saintly functions in Catholic piety. One saint relieves toothache, whereas another comforts pregnant women, and a third the shipwrecked—this amounts to a practical polytheism or henotheism. On the other hand, psychologist William James commends an imagination that tolerates so many colliding images, drawn from divergent religious experiences, unique to every person. For an orderly monistic or monotheistic system, he fears, might succumb to a craving for logical coherence, and trim rich ambiguity from the mystery.

A high percentage of my students admit using charms or spells for success in exams and athletic contests. Rummaging through his wallet, one man showed my class a small, exquisitely packaged amulet, purchased at a large Shinto shrine in Tokyo, for help in passing his bar exam. "I don't pray in any formal way to God," writes a woman athlete. "But before games, our team usually says a prayer together. I pray along, hoping that someone up there might listen. True, success is based on practice, not outside assistance. But I often put on the same socks I wore before in a really successful game, and reproduce every ritual from that event I can remember. This looks like faith or luck, but I think it is simply placing myself where the odds, and my own self-confidence, are as high as possible." Yet no American Indian brave would have proved more careful in fulfilling prescribed rites of the hunt, trying to propitiate the spirits of each dead animal, so that the quarry next time would still be plentiful.

The recent Nobel Prize poet Derek Walcott, from a devout Caribbean Methodist background, locates the subtle rudiments of prayer behind many of these idiosyncratic rituals of preparation. The creation of a poem has something votive, humble, and ritualistic about it. The descent into a sort of creative trance comes from God, and it cannot be forced. Individual writers develop characteristic postures and attitudes as they stare at their blank paper. "And in a sense, without doing it, they are crossing themselves. I mean, it's like the habit of some Catholics going into the water—you cross yourself before you go in. Any serious attempt to try to do something worthwhile is ritualistic."[7]

The Diabolic and Daimonic

Though many of my students and clients have a rich middle-zone imagination, and believe in ghosts, only a handful report actual experiences of the devil. At any rate, to control demons or harmful impersonal forces, most religious traditions make provision for saintly intermediaries, summoned by unusually effective prayer and ritual. One student, a real estate agent, writes of the refusal by successive Chinese clients to purchase a house rendered taboo by the landlord's recent suicide. Eventually this agent had to pay the fee of a Taoist exorcist in Chinatown, who later posted a certificate to mark the building's spiritual fumigation.

Filipino Catholics customarily invite the priest to bless their new house or apartment, a rite many believe will protect the family from all haunting ghosts and devils. The ceremony consists in a procession of all the guests from room to room, marked by blessings for every nook with holy water and a few lines of prayer. When I am invited as a priest to perform an occasional house dedication, I do ask a blessing, not so much for the house as for the home and people in it. But I edit from the prayers any hint of banishing an actual devil. Though I appreciate the imaginative power of such a symbol, I have learned it serves too often as yeast for religious paranoia, a counterfeit to be analyzed later in chapter 5. It is important, especially among fellow Catholics, that no word or gesture of my own be misread as promoting this counterfeit. Moreover, my own private faith has no room for a literal devil existing outside the human mind.

In exploring the religious middle zone, many anthropologists, historians of religion, and religious counselors do not hesitate to understand diabolic symbols, just as the devotee interprets them. This is a correct attitude of disciplined empathy, not imposing one's own religious forms, but opening oneself to the way people view themselves. Moreover, dualism has always been with us—God and Satan, Christ and Anti-Christ, Buddha and Mara, superego and id. Despite efforts at openness, my own modified two-tiered view of the cosmos is busy deconstructing the Satan symbol in one of three ways. What goes by the name of Satan is just some unrecognized ambivalence in a person's own unconscious life. Or parapsychological energies exist that have not yet been charted by the experimental sciences. Or yearning to express a link somehow between two mysteries, God and human evil, people end up mistaking their bipolar metaphors for a literal dualism.

The psychological basis for belief in devils can be grasped better if interpreted in the context of "Turn of the Screw," the popular tale by Henry James. Here the governess narrator, a sensitive consciousness with lightning intuitions, attributes to Miles and Flora an almost miraculous innocence from the moment of her first encounter with these children. Guided by this preconception, she rules out their potential for pranks and disobedience, which most parents would take for granted. When both children's mounting truancies at last become unmistakable, she has to blame someone outside themselves. And since no other human being is present, she reasons that the source must be evil spirits. However, two major premises of the governess must be called into question. She is prone to view children too idealistically. And as a consequence, she expects to locate the source of evil outside rather than inside.

Many reports of diabolic possession seem propped up by these same two premises. At times the two-tiered imagination limits its scope only to a genial God, confronted by a human person spotless and born-again. If so, then any acts of rebellion and sin tend to be credited to some manipulative outside source, even to evil personified. Scholars commonly trace the Satan myth in Jewish, Christian, and Muslim texts back to historical Persian sources, a political model of absolute despotism. Rebellion against such a monarch was inconceivable, an upheaval of chaos against righteousness. Titanic and malevolent, this Satan rebel dwells outside the religious cosmos. On the other hand, figures like Coyote in American Indian myth, or playful Monkey in Chinese myth, stemming from less monolithic sources, include alongside or even within the Sacred a measure of independence, trickery, and mischievous revolt.[8]

Instead of this Satan figure, the Trickster is my obvious preference, suggesting all the ambiguous, unresolved aspects in both an individual's self-concept and god-concept. This is the inner creative *daimon* of Socrates and Goethe, or the Abraxas god-image of Jung and Herman Hesse—a balance of threatening and also benign forces. As psychologist Rollo May suggests, the daimonic consists of those complexes or unmanageable urges you tend to deny in yourself and project onto others. It is anything that threatens and can at times take control of you. For example, it could be anger, sexuality, or craving for power.

The aim in therapy, and even more so, in later stages of spiritual transformation, is not to exorcise a concrete satanic presence from the possessed individual. Each person is guided instead to repossess vital drives that have been estranged and externalized, perhaps through anxiety, self-righteous disdain, or ignorance. The rejected component that haunts and punishes must be integrated back again as part of the complete personality. It may then become a new source of religious power.[9]

Case of the Man Afraid of Statues

Only an extended case study can paint a convincing religious context for daimonic forces, or for a therapeutic attempt at repossession instead of conventional exorcism. The following narrative about fear of statues, besides summing up the major topics in this chapter, offers evidence of a gifted daimonic religious imagination.

Dino, as I shall call him, was in his late twenties, tall and sinewy, dressed in a conservative tweed jacket and tie. After phoning the psychology department to ask specifically for a priest counselor, he had at last been passed along to me, and we agreed to meet for an initial interview at the Jesuit community residence. Though given a sketch of his problem on the phone, I was not prepared for his distraught reaction as I approached him at the reception desk.

Sweating heavily, shrinking from the receptionist, trying to shield his eyes from some calamity, the man reached out to grab my arm with relief, even before we shook hands in introduction. "Spooked out," was his reiterated phrase to describe the anxiety. He recounted his nervous efforts to slip into the front entrance, without crossing too near a life-sized statue of Francis of Assisi, popular target of pigeons and sparrows in a small garden shrine opposite the doorway. The next tripwires were large portraits of the pope and the archbishop of San Francisco near the desk. All the images seemed so ominous, that he wondered how to creep by these lions in the path to keep his appointment.

Almost everyone experiences some forebodings at first contact with a counselor. But the symptoms this man displayed, and his first animated explanation, embodied these misgivings in an especially histrionic way. Perhaps the key word here is embodied. In the first and subsequent sessions, I grew progressively more aware of his tendency to embody everything. Each major thought and feeling he disclosed was accompanied by jackhammer, angular body language, and his vocabulary was very tactile. You could anticipate his comprehension or dissent at any stage of discussion by the sudden eagerness in his eyes, a quizzical grimace, or an impatient shift in his seating position.

Since Dino came primarily to disclose a history of panic reactions to religious images, and his immediate behavior acted out this anxiety at first hand, I began to formulate a proposal toward the end of our first session. Would he care for a tour of St. Ignatius Church next door, or lunch in the Jesuit dining room? Both sites had a profusion of statues and paintings, I explained, and we could either set these hurdles as later goals in therapy, or else try them out now, perhaps to demystify their menace. Unable to cope with a dark church, he opted for lunch, because he thought the relaxed setting would offset any threat from images in the dining room.

Dino was brave in this first decision, for he had to check out each new picture frame that flashed by in our passage along two narrow corridors to enter the dining room, and then a few more wall images near our table. I could hear him coach himself in a nervous undertone, "Well now, here we are—just another picture, aren't you? No problem here!" He had to creep up on each one, before it could take him by surprise. Observing these habitual strategies of his, one by one, I began to imagine various behavioral therapy techniques that could build readily on his own repertoire of defenses.

That day and in subsequent sessions, Dino told his story. An accountant with a large firm, still studying for certification exams, he was the youngest of five in a devout Catholic Italian-American family, all of whom had been educated for at least twelve years in parochial schools. The first year of high school, given an option to live with either his mother or father after their divorce, he chose his mother, mostly because she seemed the more reliable and communicative of the two. He had won a basketball scholarship to college, but could not impress the coach sufficiently to make first string, so he ended up funneling more time into college studies than any year before.

Despite his panic attacks, which had just begun at the end of college five years ago, he thought himself relatively happy with his career. Though he truly loved a young woman, he was not yet ready to marry. The only prominent failures in his life, as he could now assess them, were three: the break-up with another girlfriend years before, and his inability to win the affection or respect of his father and the college basketball coach. I single out these disappointments because of their relevance to our later sessions. Such losses, he felt, had been turned into compensations, for he now valued friendships more, and tried harder, sometimes too hard, to be a likable person.

Suddenly a few years ago, he had begun to panic in the presence of large statues, which seemed peering from above or behind him, whenever he entered a church. He could associate no specific inciting event with this abrupt change in experience. Ever since childhood, Dino had never questioned his family religious heritage, and still felt a close relationship with God, with whom he liked to converse on regular visits to a church on his way home from work. But waiving the conventional Sunday Mass obligation, and rather lenient in his standards of sexual morality, he felt it necessary to remind me repeatedly that he was not, for instance, as solid or informed a Catholic as his elder brother. But why measure his own unique faith, I asked, alongside his brother's? He confessed a regrettable vulnerability since his earliest years to conform to others' expectations, including those of his brother and mother.

Had he experienced any other phobias now or in the past, such as fear of heights, blood, dirt, crowds? No. And had there been any earlier forecast of this anxiety about images? His memory latched onto a few vivid scenarios. At about four years old, entering a strange church with his parents, he had put a hand on the foot of some humongous statue, and looked up terrified at the glowering face. Again, once in Washington, he felt a grisly fear as he stood near the seated figure of Lincoln—dead matter, with an eerie living semblance, suggesting the middle zone of zombies and vampires.

In our later sessions, motifs of failure, guilt, and fear emerged repeatedly, because some combination of these feelings approximated the unnameable anxiety he felt toward religious images. Though he had always shown confident strength in combat throughout childhood and afterwards, he admitted even now an irrational terror that someone might come from behind and try suddenly to strangle him. I wondered if any family member or friend, in playful affection or cruelty, had frightened him habitually or even once. Yes, he said. This same elder brother and Dino often used to surprise and scare each other in the cellar.

I asked if he had considered avoiding those churches with statues and images that spooked him, or more practical yet, staying away from churches altogether. He took offense at this suggestion, for he cherished religious sculpture and painting—the more profuse and colorful, the better. "My emotional Latin temperament, you know," he joked. Also, he insisted I must not even hint that he attend church less often. Moreover, I must agree to challenge his relaxed version of Catholicism if I ever thought anything about it wrong or illogical. For Dino loathed shallow moral relativism and chose a priest psychologist precisely so that his faith would be supported and challenged, not watered down. I had no trouble accepting these conditions. But in the earlier sessions, I did not want to risk diverting attention from the demanding work of therapy to an exploration of religious issues. Instead, we concentrated on a direct behavioral attack against his panic symptoms.

Confronting the Daimonic

To prepare for a few desensitization exercises, I asked Dino to take colored snapshots of every threatening statue and icon he could remember in the city, and also to bring me iconography books with comparable samples. In the meantime, I taught him systematic relaxation techniques, in which he would lie flat on a couch and then slowly tense and relax his arms, facial muscles, neck, back, chest, legs, all in a ritual pattern. After this routine, he would try to locate which parts of his body still felt tight or uncomfortable. Then after working further on these special zones, he would broach a trance-like condition, trying to imagine a beach scene of silence and peace. His earlier athletic experience with visualization exercises helped him immeasurably here. Years before, in my own counselor training, one supervisor had introduced me to these operant conditioning methods, which now seemed the obvious style of therapy to match Dino's situation.

The program we agreed upon had some calculated effects. The desensitizing scale tries to accustom a person to ascend from a manageable stimulus to a progressively more demanding one—for example, from a religious image slightly menacing to one of pure terror. Controlled relaxation ought to help him cope with his increasing anxiety as we ascend the scale, always ready to fall back to a restful plateau of achievement, each time the climb proves too stressful. By tracking down the snapshot locations, Dino would in that very process be demystifying his data, now handling it according to the measure of a photographer, art critic, detective, or self-therapist. He and I would be working together in a coaching relationship, a familiar situation in his sports background, both of us lined up against his defined problem. Also, since a crucial ingredient in his panics had been lack of conscious control, he would be learning through exercises in bodily relaxation, active imagination, and retrieval of the fearful data, how increasingly to resume control.

In the desensitizing exercises we would sit in adjacent chairs, and for instance, slowly page through sections he had marked in a large art book on Medieval and Renaissance religious iconography. Moving slowly from less to more frightful images, he insisted in our first experiments on turning the pages himself. The sweat glistening on his forehead, his breathing convulsive, he would cautiously sidle up to each example, with muttered self-inducements. Whenever he slammed into an image too difficult to handle, I would ask him to stop, locate the anxiety in his body, and perform relaxation rituals at the chair or office couch.

Both of us would also discuss stylistic or iconographic details of each disturbing image, and try to fathom the basis for its particular spell. At times he would revert to easier items in the sequence, to restore his morale. Had he been wired for biofeedback tests, surely the needle would register swift changes in pulse, temperature, skin tension, and other bodily indications. Gradually he permitted me alone to turn the pages, even daring me now and then to toss in a shocking specimen out of our established sequence. It became a game which evoked many skills of the competitive athlete, and he soon mastered almost any sequence we could both devise. Between weekly sessions he practiced the program at home, and in a few months he could manage without a coach.

In his snapshots and selected prints, what patterns linked the menacing images? This question never left my mind. At first I suspected the common theme would be some lurid sado-masochistic fantasy, smuggled in under the veneer of pious self-immolation. The martyred saint writhing on a gridiron. The virgin's heart, sketched with anatomical correctness, and pierced with daggers and arrows. Christ's dead body in an advanced stage of putrefaction. But these scenes did not predominate as our portfolio enlarged. I concluded that most of the disturbing art prints, and Dino's statue snapshots, seemed to specialize in gross naturalistic detail, often tactile and kinetic, with little aesthetic distance. The major subjects were God the Father, Jesus or the Sacred Heart, Mary, and a few saints.

In almost every offensive picture, the faces showed pronounced grief, perhaps disappointment or repudiation, sometimes a direct neutral stare. At last, I tried out my conjectures on Dino himself. Somehow he had offended these sacred presences in his life, I suggested, and they were now reacting with a gaze marked by regret or accusation. The more life-size and naturalistic their semblance, the more intensely could emotions in these figures register on a sensitive observer. I pointed out a particular look of disapproval or grief in this or that print. Which familiar person in his background feels this way about him? Who feels especially judgmental about Dino's moral or religious life? I was hoping, of course, for a clear, univocal target, such as the coach, his parents, or brother. But with honesty, he could only indicate the combined faces of these people and so many others he had been trying to please, often unsuccessfully.

Since his compulsion to win approval surfaced again and again as the pivotal theme, I tried to discover all I could about the ways his conscience functioned. With no prompting from me, he distinguished two ethics. There was first the faith and morality he had been taught in his Catholic legacy, emphasizing places and times for requisite Common Prayer, and a severe code of premarital chastity. But his own personal ethic stressed different values—the effort to be kind, truthful, respectful, and unselfish. God seemed approving when Dino adhered to this private individual ethic, and disapproving when he did not.

He also described a close informal prayer relationship with God, and felt eager to preserve this intimacy at all costs. His characteristic style of prayer was asking for strength to carry out God's will, or raising worrisome questions like these: "Who am I, really? Would you like me, God, if I were truly myself, or must I become someone else to please you? What can I do to please you?" We both recognized that an insecure self-image consistently affected the way Dino addressed his god-image.

At this point, I raised an important question of my own. Did he feel better about himself in adult life, whenever he attended Mass more regularly and adhered to the Catholic sexual ethic he had been taught? Yes, unquestionably. Earlier this year, during Lent, he had gone to Mass three times a week, and noted an improved self-image. The pragmatist in me suggested that Dino try an experiment for a few weeks. Why not return to the exacting religious and moral practices of his earlier Catholic formation, and then see if the panic reaction to images diminished?

The intent of my recommendation, of course, would be just to test out a hypothesis. As a result of this experiment, he might well decide to reject or affirm his Catholic ethic with new self-understanding. More explicitly, I pressed him to compare the ethic of his public religious heritage with the private ethic he was now actually living, and probe with care which of the two represented his own authentic conscience. I reminded Dino of his earlier insistence that he counted on me for an undiluted religious challenge. But at the same time I could not encourage him to violate his genuine adult conscience—maybe regressing permanently to an earlier, more extrinsic phase of moral development, just to get rid of a few panic attacks. His religious images might have turned their faces against him for dismissing a few outgrown taboos, or more important, for turning against his true conscience, the inexorable law of gravity. Only Dino himself could discern the answer.

Within a month he had decided his frightening images were associated with taboos of Catholic folk wisdom, not with his mature individual conscience. He had been living a split-level existence. The upper floor contained stock censorious images of God and the saints, associated with a strict conventional ethic. The ground floor contained a friendly god-image, correlating with his own flexible moral values. However, though he could no longer endorse second-level taboos, he had no intention of abandoning that level's familiar heritage of Catholic images. So he was determined to live on the ground level alone and bring the demons and haunting ghosts of the abandoned attic downstairs. He intended to continue his desensitizing exercises and master them.

One day he reached a fundamental insight in his own way, during a routine question of mine about Dino's experience of God's nearness or distance. I corrected my phrase, explaining that it is we, of course, who move close or distant—our imagination of God, not God himself. This triggered a dramatic reversal of consciousness: "Yes, I myself am the one who moves away from God," he exclaimed. "God does not move away from me. He does not point his finger at me to condemn, but I fail my own values, I accuse myself. If my own imagination has the power to bring on panic attacks, it also has the power to stop them!"

Not long after this we both agreed that he would manage the desensitizing program on his own, without formal sessions. But he promised to contact me periodically, as he sensed the need. Six months later, he dropped in to share a strategic, powerful visualization exercise he had concocted. The garish details, to use his own phrase, at first "spooked me out." He would lie relaxed in bed at home, willing the most drastic religious images to exert their power on him. Often nothing happened. But at times he could feel the old tension and sweat as their presence hovered over his body. At the feverish extremity of this experience, he would imagine tearing open his chest and exposing all his insides.

According to his own interpretation, this ritual symbolized his own authentic ethic, asserting its power against the superimposed ethic of his Catholic tradition. Then he would try to sustain and repeat this experience, until its energy dissipated. At last, letting all the fantasies sputter away, he would feel a remarkable peace. This style of self-therapy had Dino's characteristic trademark—the tactile, gory props, a titanic combat, all the garish spookery of his earlier nightmares. I wagered that his custom-built cure would prove effective, at least for his presenting problem. Like the early Christian desert ascetics, he had become a champion of the spirit, flexing his daimonic imagination, mastering the worst ordeals.

Basic Religious Parallels

Dino's visualization experience stands in my memory as a baroque rite of repossession or reintegration. An exorcism therapy would have meant expelling the images either from his Catholic attic, or worse, his own ground floor. But repossession therapy meant an attempt to reconcile both floors, or to give the religious images a new configuration. His entire therapy experience dramatizes the interacting three dimensions of any religious experience, mentioned at the beginning of this chapter—universal, cultural, and individual. There are recognizable common archetypal patterns, a specific Catholic legacy of images, including those of the middle zone, and his own displaced or reintegrated individual daimon.

His final initiation rituals evoke scenarios from the world's nuptial mystics, wounded by God's arrows, or ripping open their body to exchange God's heart for their own. Jacob is said to have engaged in a fierce wrestling contest with an angel of the Lord. In some accounts of Muhammad's visionary ascent to heaven, he is awakened one night by angels, who prepare him for the journey by splitting open his chest, taking out his heart, and purifying it in water. Many shamanic trance experiences recount a comparable series of ordeals: demons and ancestral spirits cut up the body, tear the eyes from their sockets, strip flesh from the bones, and insert new blood, new flesh. This is the shaman's initiatory death and resurrection.

In my vivid therapy experience with Dino, we both gained new insight into uncharted forces of the religious imagination. But centuries before, the Tibetan Book of the Dead had shrewd anticipations of almost every step we managed to travel. When you leave your body at death, the text cautions, and approach nirvana, or else a threshold awaiting your next earthly reincarnation, do not be afraid of angry god-images that bar your passage and scream at you. "This is what you have to hear because you turned a deaf ear to the saving truths of religion! All these forms are strange to you, you do not recognize them for what they are. They terrify you beyond words, and yet it is you who have created them." These are just dream images, "which you project outside, without recognizing them as your own work."

Condensing the wise psychology in this tradition into a few verses, the sacred book concludes: "It is you yourself who pronounce your own judgment, which in its turn determines your next rebirth. No terrible God pushes you into it. You go there quite on your own."[10]

4

The Way and Its Detours

Thus far in this study a few definite religious counterfeits have surfaced. Conformism and literalness, for instance, may impair the Common Prayer tradition. Or hankering for materialistic favors can distort genuine communion with the dead. By applying the term *counterfeit* to these examples, it is possible to recognize a recurring situation. Here an individual's nominal religious identity is undercut by habitual attitudes that contest or caricature that identity. Between face value and actual worth there is a mismatch, a lack of psychological and religious integration.

As mentioned before, integration implies a religious-psychological dialectic: two distinct but inseparable dimensions, both needing each other for completeness. Roughly synonymous terms like completeness, full humanness, integration, maturity, and individuation—all these imply not an achieved plateau, but an ever converging process.

The religious factor has been described as that center in one's life which gives it ultimate coherence, and the ideal spiritual person as someone living a more or less religiously integrated life. The process of religious integration implies a constant reach beyond dependence and self-centredness, beyond a moral vision limited just to one's immediate ego or clan. Not just a random lapse, but any habitual pattern of blocking, reversing, sidetracking, parodying this religious growth process shall be designated a religious counterfeit. Insofar as it spells disorder, imbalance, or immaturity, the counterfeit can be partial or extreme, depending on each individual context.

This lack of inner integration may be so nuanced that it defies immediate recognition. Some years ago, I was impressed by the strenuous spirituality of one young college student. Member of the Baptist Student Union, prominent in every pro-life or anti-nuclear boycott, she helped run a local soup kitchen for the homeless. After class I once complimented her on a flawless exam. But she startled me with a sudden burst of tears and began hinting how much these efforts cost her. A story of self-torment and guilt unfolded.

By now she was questioning her ability to handle the tireless demands around her. Youngest in a family of six, her father's pet, she had grown up ashamed to be exempted from whippings dealt the other five, who resented her immunity. In their family album, her face so outnumbered the others that she would rip out snapshots to rectify the imbalance. By now her life had become an endless pirouette, desperate to please, mediate, play the mascot or scapegoat.

What passed for devoted Christian activism, then, felt so precarious. She sensed a huge flaw in herself, like an encroaching geological fault.

Surely this woman's Christian faith was sincere. But her situation prompts a few conjectures. Suppose she agreed to a battery of diagnostic tests, such as the MMPI, CPI, and Rorschach. No testing method could be acceptable, of course, that belittled the overt religious factor as prima facie immature.

Should therapy be recommended, then, it would proceed on the following assumptions. At present her own implied religious center is minimally integrated with the rest of her life. Drawing on her Baptist heritage, she tends to overstress, even distort selected attitudes, symbols, and rites from this tradition that rationalize her disorder. You could guess the sort of religious counterfeits that would play up to her particular character style and developmental history. And if she were to turn to other historical religious traditions, too, you could predict features in each legacy conducive to her particular disorder.

The present chapter is divided into two sections about obstacles on the quest toward religious integration. The first part introduces the more extreme breakdowns or detours, and probes for whatever religious framework still functions there. The later section, dealing with partial disorders, offers a preliminary sketch of three classical Ways to the sacred, each with its distinctive counterfeits. The ensuing chapters 5, 6, and 7 each study one of these Ways in depth.

Breakdown, Breakthrough

Chapter 1 quarreled over the readiness of some psychologists to pin tags of mental disorder on every religious experience. Yet their bias, on the other hand, does have some credibility. For the traces of madness, disease, criminality, artistic genius, and religious fervor bear a facile resemblance, and often fuse in popular imagination. However,

I must now own up to a reverse bias—a disposition to search for the potential religious alias everywhere, even in severe mental disorders.

With the ready labels of their specialties, lawyers call a person insane, the litterateur says mad, and the psychoanalyst says psychotic. The term breakdown in this section title means any extreme mental dysfunction, such as schizophrenia or a bipolar mood disorder, diagnosed by standard psychological testing. Consistent with the approach explained so far, I shall presume a severe alienation here from the individual's implied religious center, an imbalance that may or may not be expressed by conventional religious symbols of guilt, alienation, or diabolic possession.

A second presumption is more controversial than the first. What an individual perceives as a breakdown is actually a potential breakthrough, a religious rite of passage, left permanently or temporarily incomplete. Just as psychologist Otto Rank defined the neurotic as a failed artist or hero, so I shall describe the breakdown victim as a failed religious visionary. The limited human mind can take reality only in measured doses, guarding against the shock of overload. Thus, each person has to develop unique tactics of selective inattention, shielding and concealing, a sort of compromise with everyday pressures. But the defenses of a schizophrenic, for instance, long burdened with more anxiety and helplessness than the average person, are desperate and less durable.[1]

Breakthrough implies an awareness of passage, daunting or terrifying, through the relatively impermeable boundaries of ordinary consciousness, the character defenses. As the mind expands beyond, it gropes for any imagery and language to gain a foothold before the progressively widening mystery. The vision becomes a quest to the ends of the earth or into uncharted caverns of the unconscious mind, an ascent to the empyrean, a descent into hell, an awakening or rebirth, an ever more intense exposure to ultimate light or fire or love, a stripping away of every hindrance between oneself and absolute Nothingness. Each metaphor or archetype falls short, but all of them gesture toward a gradual refiguration of consciousness, shifting toward integration or completion.

You can distinguish two essential stages in this visionary quest. First, there is the prophetic departure from normal social order, which the majority will treat as deviant or revolutionary. Second, there is the crucial initiation experience itself, goal of the quest, followed by at least an attempted return to ordinary consciousness. These two motifs will now be developed more fully.

Prophetic Departure

Who is normal? The people judged most sane in any society are usually the majority, shaped mostly by the unquestioned values of that culture. The minority are often perceived as deviant. As indicated in chapter 2, the average religious insider, dulled to self-criticism, tends to discount the outsider as nameless. Yet the majority, eager to discredit nonconformity under labels of disease or fraud, often prove color-blind to the pathology of conformity. They forget that a consensus in any society can be undermined, not just by transgressing it, but by embodying it to excess, and to absurdity.

Freud, for instance, transcends his own patriarchal limitations at times by challenging the bourgeois verities of his era. His typical Viennese businessman would seek psychoanalysis, not for himself, but for a depressed wife or unruly children. Society treated this successful, fiercely competitive gentleman as a paragon of normalcy. Yet Freud suspects the man unconsciously wants his family recycled only to comply with his perverse authority, the actual source of their present mental affliction. The therapist is paid to send them back into a family or social milieu that itself subverts the cure. Freud conjectures that some epochs, even entire cultures, might be neurotic. Outside this relativistic hall of mirrors, he wonders if there exists any objective criterion of sanity.[2]

In every historical period, the vintage counter-culture and the art of asylums are sometimes indistinguishable. Most therapists soon learn respect for the garish dreams and hallucinations of the seriously disturbed. For what the majority in a society perceive as confused dribble on a Jackson Pollock canvas can yield its own tricky emotional logic. You find evidence that leading surrealists and expressionists, such as Kokoschka, Klee, or Dali, often studied the art of asylums. Like the paintings of children and Primal societies, so this mad art offered new techniques to break from conventional mindsets. Thus, Dali could veer toward the edge of normalcy to meet the schizophrenic artist. And the latter, perhaps through the therapy of art, could veer toward the edge of abnormality, approaching the normal.

A favorite theme in literature is the revolutionary wisdom of the mad. The Fool's riddles and mummery in *King Lear,* Lucky's single raving monologue in *Waiting for Godot,* the idiot Benjy's serene perspective in *Sound and the Fury*—these passages become the work's most sensitive register, calling the majority consensus into question. You are persuaded to join the heroes of Heller's *Catch-22* and De Broca's film *King of Hearts* in an asylum, rather than fight society's crazy wars outside. All these impulsive, dissident characters recall the trickster figures of American Indian folklore, the jester who holds up a fearless mirror of ridicule at court, or the archetypal holy fool of Russia. Their insane or irreligious antics act as a spur of prophetic intensity. The cultural majority are sent back to reexamine conventional dividing lines between genuine sanity or genuine faith on one hand, and their counterfeits on the other.

A similar reversal of focus often occurs in family therapy, when a counselor is asked to aid the individual designated by remaining members as disturbed. This selected member sometimes proves to be the family scapegoat, more balanced than the rest, someone unable or unwilling to adjust as readily as the others to a harmful network of relationships. In one family of recent immigrants from southern Europe, for example, a frail ten year old girl had begun skipping her grade school classes, hiding under beds, refusing to talk. As an excuse for this behavior, she claimed classmates were bullying her. During one session including her father, mother, and two younger brothers, I happened to ask her, "Won't your father protect you?" "Look at my dad," she smiled, pointing. "He's so silly, and so nice, he couldn't protect anyone!"

Her father later confided that he had lost himself in an obsessive extramarital affair. To this outrage the wife reacted with overly dependent feelings toward both sons, and so her daughter ended up excluded and unloved. Thus, half-aware of her symbolic behavior, the young girl, hiding under beds, was perhaps acting out a masque of premature entombment. Before any help can be offered a family like this, their unique values must first be studied as an isolated culture in microcosm. The odd criteria of deviance need an audit and confrontation.

In some situations, what looks like religious blasphemy or heresy is actually a sound weapon against the tyranny of parents. *Voices Calling,* the story of Lisa Wiley's schizophrenic breakdown, tells how her mother imprinted on the child a tight moral code, with punishments for swearing or slang. "Firm faith in God," Lisa writes of this woman, "made her believe her children would be protected from any serious trouble. For she had always been a faithful servant to the Lord."

Lisa attends a church camp one summer with reluctance, just to please her mother. And there she experiences some of her first hallucinations, a siege of crackling and sputtering in the brain. At the very instant of asking God for a clean heart, her mind would spew out words attributed to the devil. "I made a man out of God and spit on him, kicked him and beat him. It was a joy to see him fall back helpless as I beat him, and I laughed and hissed inwardly . . . I knew I was guilty but was unable to care.'' Maybe her first stumble toward an autonomous conscience, Lisa's words bravely defy an imposed religion, and more important, the smothering authority of her mother.[3]

A paranoid schizophrenic patient, whom I used to visit in a psychiatric unit, once explained the behavior that prompted his family to confine him. Neighbors complained to police about an obscene tableau mounted on the prominent roof-deck of his posh colonial residence. Throughout December, a Santa dummy of King Kong proportions sprawled there, one hand clutching a gin bottle, its head missing, the body a pin cushion of javelins and swords. Reams of tickertape spiraled around Santa's reindeer, decked with ad posters, jockstraps, and brassieres. But this high-income neighborhood insisted on shielding its children from such gross exhibitionism. With the pain of an unappreciated author, the patient now sat in a locked ward, giving a commentary on each symbol in this montage.

The man had designed a flamboyant protest against the commercialization of Christmas. I thought his work could pass for creative social commentary if offered in modeling clay or acrylic at a museum of modern art. He sounded that day like an adept New Critic, explicating an especially creative dream, or like a prophet, outraged at debasement of a Christian feastday.

Yet despite its imaginative impact, the schizophrenic breakdown of people like this patient or Lisa Wiley must never be romanticized. Not the sense of engulfment and loss, the harrowing depression, the capacity to harm. Recent anti-psychiatry militants argue that many asylum inmates might be richly endowed human beings, locked up for disputable social reasons. This slant takes extreme form in Philippe De Broca's *King of Hearts,* for instance, a major cult film of the psychedelic sixties. Measuring the insanity of a warring society alongside insanity in an asylum, the film sides with gentle inmates staging a festival in costumes from an abandoned circus. The fantasy asylum is an Arcadia of humane amusements, such as bike riding, card playing, and dancing. It bears no hint of the actual mental horror.

The Classical Prophets

The disturbed Christmas tableau of my artistic friend suggests any number of parallel scenarios featuring the world's great religious eccentrics. Foremost in mind is an image of Samuel and the earliest wandering Hebrew prophets—drunk on God, possessed by the Lord's *ruah* or life-force. Even the later prophet Jeremiah is directed in one of his visions to buy a linen loincloth, wear it in public, hide it in a crevice of rocks, and after some delay dig up the spoiled remains. Once he has acted out this dumb-show, Jeremiah conveys God's own interpretation: "Thus will I spoil the gross pride of Judah . . . Just as a loincloth is bound close to a man's waist, so I bound all Israel and all Judah to myself. . . . But they did not listen" (13:9-11).

Similar tales of defiant charade occur among seers and mystics of the East. The Taoist Chuang-tzu introduces the wise king Po Chu, who performs an extraordinary ritual over the corpse of an executed criminal. Descending from his throne, he wraps the body in his own royal robes and then grieves aloud. More than the rest of us, this criminal has suffered the cruelties of our world: "They pile on responsibilities, and then penalize people for not being able to fulfill them."

Echoing the tradition of Taoist seers and anarchists, with their skirmishes against Confucian orthodoxy, the popular Zen masters delight in provocative slaps and kicks to shatter a disciple's equanimity. Though the sacred is conceived by Jews, Christians, and Muslims as a transcendent presence, distinct from the human intermediary, it becomes a more immanent power in most prophets of the East. An enhancing aura, charisma, or uncanny gaze lend intense authority to their words. This is especially true of the Hindu reformer Gandhi, sweeping away hallowed certainties of religious caste, ritual animal slaughter, child marriage, and spurning the extortionist conversion tactics of Christian missionaries.

To many people today, the notion of religion first connotes sanity, the conservative status quo, institutions acting as baby sitter for the young, solace for the handicapped, superego for the delinquent. Yet its more radical shadow-image is strangely overlooked. During Paul's trial in the Acts of the Apostles, Festus, the Roman governor, combines charges of political sedition and religious heresy into a simple accusation: "Paul, you are raving. Much study is driving you mad!" This is the same insanity Paul in First Corinthians describes as the divine folly, which picks out the world's weak and outcast, fools, mere nothings, to overthrow all that the world thinks wise. William James calls this madness the theopathic paradox of the saints.

Like other world traditions, Christian history has its own stream of mad deviants: early martyrs whom the deified Roman emperor viewed as atheists, monastic communities that withdrew from a complacent Christian society, persecuted Anabaptist radicals of the Protestant Reformation, or the outspoken Latin American theologians of liberation. In our own era both religious and irreligious catchwords are invoked by tyrants and also by revolutionaries. Thus, the religious factor must always be treated as potentially dialectical. At times it supports, even absolutizes given social norms. But other times it becomes a religion of the oppressed, offering people in that society an ultimate basis on which to question and overturn any penultimate certainty.

Initiation Complete and Incomplete

After abandoning defenses, social approval, and everyday consciousness, the person subjected to breakdown or breakthrough next faces a harrowing initiation into the mystery. The second stage of this visionary quest now commences. Its atmosphere is conjured vividly by Mircea Eliade and Joseph Campbell: a long, deep retreat inward into the soul, backward in time. A series of dark terrifying experiences. If the candidate is fortunate, encounters soon occur that fulfill, harmonize, center, and give new courage. This pattern is the Joycean monomyth, prevalent in so many folk tales and the classical epics. A hero or heroine leaves the everyday world and enters a region of sacred wonder, encounters fabulous powers, wins a decisive victory, and returns to share the treasure of vision or wealth with those at home.[4]

Perhaps the clearest religious prototype of this quest experience is the sacred hunting rite of Primal cultures. Here rituals are devised to prepare hunters for their departure from society, and to produce medicine and spells for outwitting the prey. Other rites purify the returning hunter after dangerous contact with the magic of slain animals. Another pervasive figure among many world traditions is the shaman, whose controlled ecstatic trance is also marked by rites at start and finish. The healer's soul leaves for a mythical journey to sky, underworld, or metaphysical center. The intent of this quest is to guide the recent dead, to cure a long-unappeased hungry ghost or a soul threatening to drift loose from its diseased body, or to search out clairvoyant spirits for knowledge about the future.

Once completed, the social implications of a shaman's journey must be shared and integrated. Special attention is given to final moments of the quest in West African traditional medicine. The Yoruba healer expects those cured of mental disorders to confirm this ritual re-entry of their sick spirit back into the body. In an elaborate rite of dismissal, patients perform a blood sacrifice to ward off any recurrence of mental breakdown, and immerse themselves in purifying waters to symbolize the completed process of rebirth.[5]

However, a visionary quest that does not, at least potentially, include this re-entry moment may be a religious counterfeit, or an immature or premature religious experience. But in my opinion, it should never be mistaken for the religious ideal. Boundaries between the ordinary and extraordinary, once transcended, are at last to be reconstituted in the light of new wisdom. This is no doubt what Teresa of

Avila means when she advises interrupting your ecstasy if a needy brother or sister asks for a cup of water. Or the Hindu mystic Sri Ramakrishna, addressing his favorite goddess Kali, begs her, "Mother, don't make me unconscious through the knowledge of Brahman. . . . Let me remain in contact with people. Don't make me a dried-up ascetic. I want to enjoy your sport in the world." Even though Ramakrishna believes the world is nothing but Brahman or Kali, he still wants to immerse himself in the earthy maya disguises of God.[6]

Gautama the Buddha determines to come back, too, from his nirvana experience beneath the Bo tree, and as a bodhisattva, vows to share the dharma with all other living creatures. An oft-cited Zen koan commends this same return from enlightenment to the immediacy of everyday life. "At first tea is sheer tea, then it is no longer tea, but at last it is indeed tea." You begin with a meditative departure from the prosaic "sheer tea," to some transcendental experience. But what still remains is the completed return—reincorporating this deeper awareness back into the concrete particular "tea indeed!"

The tragic impact of schizophrenia and most other serious disorders is that of a failed or gravely disrupted crossing back, over broken boundaries of the self, to ordinary consciousness. Unlike great religious mystics, the mentally afflicted lack training in prolonged meditation and self-induced trance, or they miss the helpful rituals, social reassurance, or conceptual framework to master the risks of re-entry. Some psychologists claim that a schizophrenic episode, no matter what its chemical or developmental causes, will often work itself out by its own laws. It aims at eventual self-healing and rebirth. Yet "what needs to be explained," as psychologist Gregory Bateson remarks, "is the failure of many who embark upon this voyage to return from it."[7]

Re-Entry: Two Case Studies

The ambushes against complete return from a schizophrenic condition are recounted persuasively in *I Never Promised You a Rose Garden,* a fictional rendering of Joanne Greenberg's own experience as an inmate at Chestnut Lodge. Today we are fortunate to have portions of the treatment notes written by the author shortly after recovery, and a case presentation from the viewpoint of her therapist, Frieda Fromm-Reichmann, shortly before Reichmann's death. The adolescent girl's precocity, the heightened expectations of her family, and also an ambience of anti-semitic rejection by her classmates, all had combined to catalyze a familiar double-bind situation. She reacted, according to Reichmann, by withdrawing into loneliness and creating "a kingdom of her own, with a religion of her own, a language of her own, in which she fully lived."[8]

Greenberg's notes indicate that the gods in her kingdom were called Yrians, but familiar people from the outside world were Kaa. "I had changed the real world or what I thought the real world was and put it into the mouth of the Kaa," she explains, and "had taken what was beautiful and called it my fantasy world and put it into the mouth of the Yrians." The novel distinguishes clearly between an earlier era, when this realm of fantasy appears serene and comforting, and a later era, when it encroaches on all her time. This realm finds progressively ingenious torments to punish her for the disloyalty of trying to live in two worlds.

After each key session in which Reichmann and her client make a quantum gain in therapy, the gods hold a war council and plot a crushing relapse. Nothing is more disturbing in the novel than these personified onslaughts by her fantasy world, once a friendly bulwark for so many years, and enriched by much of her best poetry. On one level, it is possible to account for this unsteady climb back to reality by sizing up her obvious nakedness and insecurity. Discarding one defense after another, at times she attempts too much, too soon. The passages I shall now cite occur in the novel, not in her notes. "Earth's virtues had a new quantity to add to the rest—hope, the little, little Maybe. Still the earth was a place full of peril and treachery, especially for an alien." But this emphasis on her defenses does little justice to the daimonic shrieks of panic and menace each time she improves enough to transfer from a confined hospital ward to a more permissive one.

Greenberg's gods are jealous gods, or in more psychological language, her fantasy-life is so consummatory and self-enclosed that it cannot be readily integrated or retrojected back into the conscious self. "Even now, delighting in a world of rich color and odors that actually referred to what one was smelling; even profoundly in love with cause and effect, optics, sonics, motion, and time all obedient to their laws, she wondered if Yr would be a fair trade for all of it." So again and again, even during a sentence in conversation with her therapist, she would suddenly tune out, regressing "terrified into Yr, so that it closed over her head like water and left no mark of where she had entered. The surface was smooth and she was gone."

Great myths have focused on this final barrier against homecoming, and on taboos forbidding easy passage between two worlds. Once you cross the sacred threshold and begin guessing the Sphinx's riddle or competing with Turandot's suitors, you cannot back out, but must triumph or die. Orpheus returning from Hades with Eurydice, and turning back to glance at her, breaks the taboo, and loses her forever. Again, looking back with regret at Sodom, Lot's wife is turned into a pillar of salt.

A similar barrier once emerged in experiments by a student with self-induced trance. She told me about a horrifying hour in which she remained locked within this twilight. Paralyzed yet fully aware, she tried in vain to move her lips for a scream, unable to drag herself back to reality. In another situation, a former client describes the massive dikes he has been building for years to push away his schizophrenic fantasy world, which once engulfed him. He still jokes about those private "movies," daydreams nursed during his teens, which later mushroomed into lurid film clips that could stun and take over his mind for entire days. Too much energy today, however, seems diverted for vigilance against these fantasies, with little left for enjoying his family and job.

The most seriously disturbed re-entry I was privileged to observe and assist was that of a twenty-five-year-old dental student, whom I shall call Carlos. Hospitalized twice for a serious bipolar mood disorder, he was now taking the psychotropic drugs lithium and haldol to monitor dangerous swings of emotion. Lasting two hours a week for seven months, our sessions supplemented his occasional visits to a psychiatrist, with whom I had reached a helpful division of roles. Carlos acted as if possessed, in a haze of constant religious mania. He thought of himself by turns as godlike or God. He had a swirl of images and ideas, a readiness to fling away all his possessions and become a swami, a certainty he could talk any woman into bed, and also a dangerous impulse to leap off roofs and fly.

In our first meeting, his feet had been bloodied from running barefoot. Unable to sleep for four days, he feared losing consciousness most of all, because he might also snuff out this miraculous religious exaltation. Raised in a fervent Catholic Filipino-American home, he had recently steeped himself in a dozen popular books on Hindu and Buddhist spirituality. He felt certain God had sent him a vision of absolute light, sublime and calm. But this sacred moment had so shaken him that he could never return to the life he had been living before. Thus, he was calling my attention to a major barricade against re-entry.

Carlos still felt anxiety about the dental career and marriage that were descending on him much too quickly. These were a few of the apparent stresses precipitating his emotional breakdown. In the glow of his ecstasy, which he yearned to sustain, he would empty his pockets to fellow students, stop strangers to tell them they were saved, and pour out his guilt and other embarrassing secrets to the first person who could not escape him. It had become possible to read others' minds, perceive an aura around the lucky ones, and construe apocalyptic messages in chance number combinations or street signs.

Unable to wean this man away from the visions themselves, even had I wanted to, I encouraged him to integrate their visionary contents into his own habitual spirituality. He must learn to discriminate between constructive and harmful effects of his impulsive actions, both on himself and on family and friends. Should a therapist have handled Carlos' experiences any different from the visions of Ramakrishna or Teresa of Avila? As William James observes, both delusional insanity and religious mysticism arise from the same marginal regions of the mind, both tell of the same extraneous voice and mission. But their effects must be tested, and "run the gauntlet of confrontation with the total context of experience, just like what comes from the outer world of sense."[9] Both Carlos and the mystics should expect to hear the same repeated challenge from their respective spiritual guides: "So God spoke to you. What difference will this event now make in your life?"

Since my client had often pressed me to teach him various styles of meditation, we began to practice simple yoga exercises together, and informal prayer. Our sessions gradually became conversations about mystical theology, and ways to translate his disturbing experience into a new, thorough way of life. It struck me more than once that he could be playing unconsciously upon our shared spiritual interests to distance me from more vital disclosures. So as the months unfolded, and his mania drained away, I tended to ration out religious words, and to help him find immediate empirical language for describing his attitudes and options. Eventually he chose a return to his fiancée and dental career, decisions he hoped would cohere best with his new faith and healing.

Afterwards a few years passed, with almost no word from Carlos. Then one day he phoned to share a graphic dream. Vested as a shaman and guided by a Beatrice figure, he wandered through a series of mythic ordeals, each testing out spiritual and magical powers he had never before acknowledged in himself. Though tempted as always to dismiss archetypal claptrap of this sort, he thought one detail crucial enough to emphasize with me. In his dream I did not show up during the shamanic journey itself, but I stood waiting beyond the finish line, anxious to welcome him home.

Yet despite this auspicious dream later, neither Carlos nor I had ended our therapy series without some mutual misgivings. In the play

Equus by Peter Shaffer, the psychiatrist Dysart decides at last to cure Alan Strang from his destructive religious fixation. The distraught client is destined to be reinserted into a sterile society that resembles his psychiatrist's own life, without intense conviction about anything. "My desire," Dysart moans, "might be to make this boy an ardent husband, a caring citizen, a worshiper of an abstract and unifying God. My achievement, however, is more likely to make a ghost! . . . Passion, you see, can be destroyed by a doctor. It cannot be created."[10]

In a comparable way, Carlos often expressed distrust of the medication prescribed by his psychiatrist. The rapid magic of haldol and lithium might deflate this passionate mysticism of his. Jung suggests the analogy of a businessman scorched by bankruptcy, and then deciding later whether to regain his former daring, now with some salutary caution added, or else to patch up his reputation within the confines of a more limited, timid personality. Thus, after confronting the menacing forces of the wider unconscious self, what should the ego do when it returns to everyday life? Jung fears that almost everyone would repudiate the religious or psychotic vision, and return much smaller, confined, more rationalistic than before.[11]

This chapter has already described a pathology of conformity, the converse of pathological deviance. My client's own decision to return to his old fiancée and dental school looked too pat, maybe a regressive slip into the conventional. On the other hand, if today he still meditates and tries to live a transformed religious life, perhaps what is essential in his ecstasy will endure, if not its intensity.

Both the religious experience and a serious breakdown can be treated as sacred rites of passage. But breakdown is a rite left unfinished. Paralyzed by an imagination of extremity, the afflicted person needs guidance from a guru, shaman, or therapist to complete the return to reality. Someone like Carlos or Joanne Greenberg must find a broader conceptual framework to handle the overwhelming ecstatic experience. Besides encouragement and affection, they need a choice of significant rituals. A comprehensive therapy, then, attempts to complete what has been temporarily aborted. It helps transform the religiously immature or premature into an integral religious experience.

Religious Detours

Focus on the sacred quest now shifts from major breakdowns to less convulsive detours, from the exotic misfit or psychotic to the average person. Chapter 3 stressed the indispensable dialectic between a specific culture, a religious heritage, and an individual's unique religious experience. It is this hidden threefold interaction that often determines the particular features in any serious breakdown.

Some years after her confinement under Fromm-Reichmann at Chestnut Lodge, Joanne Greenberg wrote the short story "Palimpsest." Here an asylum director, Dr. La Doux, ponders the radical change in psychotic styles during his own lifetime. He imagines that each Bastille prisoner in solitary confinement, isolated from other prisoners by walls too thick to transmit the tap of a message, suddenly omits standard words or coins new ones. In a comparable way, today hysteria fades, but anorexia and depression are rampant. Catatonic schizophrenia has almost vanished, explained away as if it had never existed. Raging Napoleons are not so common as before. Symptoms and metaphors are discarded or sewn in new lengths. "Who sends the message that sets the style?" La Doux questions. "Where on the outside is the consensus made that sets the Bastille singing its songs, adding new verses and dropping old ones?"[12]

The same cultural influences that mould the dramatic symptoms in an asylum also affect the religious maturation of us all, far more than we imagine. Humanity contains in itself an immense range of potential character types and behavior. But each culture, each historical period, selecting among these possibilities, will standardize its particular choice. The identity chosen by an individual may not be the one most congenial. People are often driven to a disastrous compromise between unique individual aspirations and the dominant social identity favored by their own subculture or family. The introvert may be pressured, for example, to become a Kiwanis toastmaster, ever more alienated from a society overrun by competitors more suited to that role.

Thus, each time someone regresses or digresses in the quest for religious integration, that person is somehow a poet searching for metaphors to express an inner predicament. And each particular community, era, and religious tradition offers the poet's unconscious mind a limited range of images and symbolic behavior—a specific repertoire of symptoms.[13]

Sensitive to this culture-bound situation, then, it is wise to outline a few patterns of ordinary religious immaturity. Though the heap of potential counterfeits is chaotic, you can still sort out the most recurrent ones and establish a typology. Locating a given phenomenon under its accurate category will mean less than an attempt to understand the phenomenon itself. At any rate, tentative labels can be useful for sifting and organizing the chaos of human behavior. They alert the mind to genuine cultural differences most of all. Realizing these first, you can then appreciate the more remarkable distribution of personality types within and across any given cultural boundary.

Story of the Three Ways

The range of mature and immature religious attitudes described in the next three chapters will be sorted under the three ancient Hindu *margas.* These are three paths to Brahman or the sacred—comprising the spiritualities of action, affectivity, and contemplation. In popular Hindu iconography, the Way of Action is represented by the *karma yogin,* an activist with busy gestures managing liturgical, family, and civic duties. The Way of Affectivity belongs to the *bhakta,* an ecstatic troubadour chanting and dancing for the gods. The Way of Contemplation is personified in the silent *jnanin,* seated in a solitary yoga trance.

There are many reasons why I prefer to classify basic religious temperaments by this threefold typology. First, the three Ways match a traditional Jewish distinction between the activist tsaddiq, devout hasid, and talmid hadham or meditative student of Torah. Counter-Reformation Catholic spirituality, too, has always identified a characteristic Jesuit activism, Franciscan exuberant love, and Dominican contemplative study. Other parallels come to mind, including the Neoplatonist will-heart-mind categories, and psychologist Karen Horney's distinction between temperaments moving against others, toward others, and detached from others.[14]

Instead of a triadic division, some psychologists will prefer the four humours or four elements of folk medicine, the eightfold classification by Jung and Myers-Briggs, Ichazo's Enneagram, or the twelve signs of the zodiac. If applied creatively, each typology alone or in combination can prove insightful, especially for dethroning the presumption that everyone else has the same temperament as one's own.

The interacting three Ways and their potential counterfeits have been embodied imaginatively in the story "Two More under the Indian Sun" by Ruth Prawer Jhabvala.[15] It offers a resourceful single text, from which illustrations can be drawn for the next three chapters. The story opens with a mild disagreement between Margaret and her younger friend Elizabeth, both British women in love with their adopted India, some years after the Raj departure. They spend an afternoon chatting at Margaret's home, a crossroads open to the steady turn-over of house guests, now including Babaji especially, a renowned Hindu holy man. The surface narrative traces Margaret's abortive attempts to talk Elizabeth into shepherding some Tibetan orphan children on a holiday tour. At last Margaret salvages the project by inviting her old friend Babaji to join the trip under her own leadership.

The thematic center in this tale, an earnest conversation featuring Margaret, Elizabeth, and Babaji on the veranda, tests out relative merits of the three Hindu ways. It becomes clear that each character personifies a different way. "Margaret maintained that it was a matter of temperament, and that while she could appreciate the beauty of the other two ways, for herself there was no path, nor could there ever be, but that of action." Behind this dialogue and interaction, the reader is asked to examine three divergent perspectives, affecting the manner in which each individual interacts with the other two present. Gradually, the central character Margaret reveals in herself traces of the other two ways that she usually disguises by genial self-caricature.

Though underscoring the symmetrical structure of this tale, one must not reduce it to a Platonic dialogue or allegory, for in the best fictive manner, it peals away layer upon layer of complexity in at least two of its three characters. Like the character of Godbole in E. M. Forster's *Passage to India,* however, Babaji remains sketchy and opaque, an elderly Hindu mystic absent from his frigid Himalayan retreat for a warmer season at Margaret's home. A retired government officer, having long outgrown anger and other bitter passions, he now radiates a sort of smiling serenity that endears him to anyone nearby. Rocking back and forth in his chair, Babaji is never obtrusive. He offers intuitive solace for Elizabeth's distress and a dab of gentle repartee for Margaret's impatience.

Representing the Way of Affectivity, Elizabeth has been married four years to Raju, whose Indian family, at first reluctant, now really appreciate her. The two are still a honeymoon couple, fully engulfed in each other. Elizabeth enjoys him so much that often when Raju falls asleep next to her, she loves to stay awake studying details of his handsome body. Once an overly committed schoolteacher, compulsive about duties of charity, a concern long shared with Margaret, she now experiences tension between her surprising bliss centered every moment on Raju, and shame that she now lacks her former sensitivity to India's misery.

Harping on Elizabeth's eroding sense of social duty, Margaret shows herself eager to itemize Raju's obvious defects—his withheld disclosures, cruelty and hurt vanity, his impatience with Margaret's opinionated interventions, and his consequent refusal to forgive her. Elizabeth cannot bear separation from Raju to join Margaret's few days of travel with orphan children. By the last page of the story, this extravagant fondness for her husband wins some grudging comprehension and support from Margaret.

In counterbalance to Margaret's bustling proficiency in social work and her eagerness to meddle and domineer, the converse side of her personality proves more kindly and vulnerable than first impressions indicate. Margaret tells of the unique warm, candid relationship with her late husband. And later during an interlude away from the veranda and Babaji, Elizabeth learns an unsuspected secret. "You know what was my happiest time of all in India? About ten years ago, when I went to stay in Swami Vishwananda's ashram." Margaret describes the freedom and joy, without a care, as if her feet no longer touched the ground. Thus, she can now fathom the ecstasy Elizabeth feels with Raju. For the Swami laughed and joked with Margaret, and sometimes sang. During those songs, the tears came pouring down her face, but she had never been more happy.

When Margaret at last asks Babaji to accompany her on tour with the orphans, she is embracing his knee, sitting at his feet. Smiling in turn, he places his hand on her head "in a gesture of affection or blessing." Here she seems to initiate the potential recovery of her earlier ashram experience, reconciling her habitual Way of action with Elizabeth's Way of devoted joy and Babaji's Way of contemplation.

The Detour of One-Sidedness

Some Hindu psychologists teach that the further all three Ways intensify and diverge, the more authentic the practice of each is likely to become. However, as interpreted by many others, including myself, the one-sided pursuit of a single Way commonly ends up in distortion.[16] To evoke the best creative influences in all three, you must first confirm your own appropriate Way as principal aim, then subordinate the other two as essential means. As life unfolds, the Way that dominates your energetic years may yield, of course, to a different Way in the final twilight. The highest action and contemplation should be permeated by affectivity, or devout action must be the fruition of a most unwavering contemplation.

Parallel to the three margas, a neglected blueprint by Freud suggests three normal libidinal character types: the obsessional centered on superego, the erotic centered on id, and the narcissistic centered on ego. These three temperaments exist separate or in various combinations, where "one or two of the three main modes of expending libido in the mental economy have been favored at the cost of the others." The ideal personality, according to Freud, would be a combined obsessional-erotic-narcissistic personality. But the one-sided exaggeration of any dimension leads respectively to obsessional neurosis, hysteria, and psychotic ego disorders.[17]

In Jhabvala's story, too, the religious ideal implies a convergence of all three Ways, whereas the single-minded pursuit of any one Way is a religious counterfeit. Margaret's conscious philanthropy looks at first like a restless workaholic quest for power. But her apology to Elizabeth and her eventual partnership with Babaji promise more balance and peace, an expansive interdependence. As mentioned before, the story is noncommittal about Babaji. Yet perhaps his meditations will gain, too, from Babaji's personal relationship with Margaret, and from a remnant of the activism that earlier preoccupied the householder developmental stage in his life. Swayed by Margaret's acute perspective on Raju, most readers probably distrust Elizabeth's incredible submersion in her one love. Though enviable in some ways, this commitment comes off as too unilateral and dependent, conducive to Raju's abuse and, perhaps, to impending surfeit and boredom for both lovers.

Chapters 5, 6, and 7 will investigate the mature and immature manifestations of these three religious Ways. Each has its own characteristic image of the sacred—a bold intervening power for the activist, a prodigal lover for the devotee, or simply a calm enabling presence for the contemplative. The ideal in each Way will always presuppose balanced integration and inclusion. Whenever basic components in any Way are pushed to excess, they turn into religious detours or counterfeits.

5

Way of Action

Throughout the Jhabvala story recounted in chapter 4, the philanthropist Margaret embodies religious activism at its most promising, but also hazardous. She shows steel and grit in assuming control, and defining any situation in her own terms. But what her friends Babaji and Elizabeth find endearing about her is perceived as stubborn and bullying by Elizabeth's husband. Raju almost views her as a predator, with attributes of the atavistic male. Yet to Margaret's credit, she does tend to inspire most people around her. Any genuine activist, unlike the imperialist or parasitic administrator, wants to facilitate action by others. The ideal is not to hoard power, but arouse initiative in as many colleagues as possible.

The Way of Action will be introduced first in its mature spiritual embodiment. As each facet of this ideal passes into view, so will omens of its immature caricature, to be examined later in more detail. An activist counterfeit, as explained in chapter 4, means attitudes already distorted by the immature religious activist, or areas in any public religious heritage especially vulnerable to an activist distortion. The three counterfeits under scrutiny are religious self-assertion, paranoia, and obsession.

The God of Action

At best, the Way of Action means discipline and expendability, especially at the moment of decision. Every serious choice reenacts a cutting of the umbilical cord, the pain of weaning and early separation from home, all the developmental rehearsals of adult independence. To achieve the solidity of one concrete act, it is necessary to shake off the chorus of other nagging alternatives.

The renunciation demanded of an activist is described by Gandhi as *nishkama karma,* action without selfish desire. A person must be "versed in action and yet remain unaffected by it." Brooding over results leads to loss of nerve in the performance of duty. Laksmi, Hindu goddess of prosperity, appears in one popular myth as the beauty who sets down the following subtle condition for any prospective suitor: "I shall accept only that man who has no desire for me!"[1] The danger is that success, instead of being a momentary stimulus, will prove an all-absorbing tyrannical quest. This risk threatens political regimes, religious traditions, and all other human endeavors, especially at their zenith. Therefore, with some plausibility the Taoist Lao-Tzu argues that only those who have no use for leadership are fit to be entrusted with it. Diffident to rank and glory, free from compulsive inner needs, such leaders know how to rule without seeming to rule.

Chapter 4 has already distinguished two different perceptions of a prophetic mission—someone in whom the sacred is an immanent power, and someone deputized by a personal transcendent God. An activist of the second type will tend to view God in one of the following ways: God takes momentary possession of the messenger, God remains distant and does not interfere, or God and the agent act in a balanced partnership. This latter cooperative relationship between the divine and human is especially difficult to imagine. Student essays and interviews cited in chapters 2 and 3 try various ways to resolve this dilemma whenever they discuss praying for favors. How does one reach a midpoint between extremes of cringing dependence and defiant autonomy? A cry for help is perhaps the most widespread form of address to a personal God, but the quality and degree of expected help may differ radically.

One of my students, a marketing major, points up this difficulty very well: "For me, God is normally an impersonal energy, but in crises he becomes a father from whom I beg help. Am I switching gears for the convenience of my imagination? Or am I regressing back to childhood? I find myself thanking God for all sorts of trivialities—like finding a parking place. Though God makes my life possible, is God responsible for such silly details? If I don't control this attitude, I'll tend to blame God when I don't pick up the number five bowling pin." The excess feared here is overdependence and irresponsibility. In any discrepancy of status between friends, the inferior can be overwhelmed by the superior personality, and become spoiled and overconfident because of a privileged connection.

In all these student responses, you can identify a number of serious attempts to redefine the mature partnership between an omnipotent, loving God and a free activist adult.[2] A major premise in this discussion is that you pray to change your own mind, not the mind of God. For God is aware of your needs, even before they are expressed. Thus, one solution of the dilemma is to confine yourself to wordless meditation in God's presence. Or you may use words, but only those of thanks and dedication. Third, you may determine to use words of petition, but center on spiritual, not material needs; or to pray only for the needs of other people. Or turning the specific request into an open-ended commitment, you may ask only for insight into God's will, and the strength to follow it. Fifth, in a simple reversal, you may retain the petitionary structure, but try to retroject into it most of the aspirations that usually get projected. For example, "Show me how I myself can answer the requests I make of you," you might pray. "God, make me alert to the prayers of other people, and responsive to their needs."

As a final approach to this problem, you can imagine a midpoint between the extremes of dependence and autonomy, a balanced interdependence. It must be conceded that most of this concern about religious independence betrays an underlying anxiety about dependence in any form. For both exaggerated dependence and independence in adults can often be traced to earlier deprivations of a balanced nurture and dependence. One mark of maturity is precisely an ability at times to consult, lean, relax, and let down one's defenses. To admit ontological dependence on God does not diminish the individual in a sort of zero-sum relationship, nor expose oneself to God's busy-body intrusions. Perhaps God, like a perceptive teacher or counselor, realizes a person needs help, and preferring not to intervene unasked, hesitates until requested willingly.

Three activist disorders will now come into focus. Each in its own way veers off from the disciplined balance sought by Gandhi and Lao-Tzu, and distorts this interdependent partnership with a personal God.

Religious Self-Assertion

The widow Margaret in Jhabvala's story gives intimations of this first imbalance, a single-minded pursuit of glory and mastery. She expands beyond limits, usurping the very space yielded by her friend Elizabeth, who herself is too ready to comply and diminish. This self-aggression echoes the audacity of Prometheus against the gods, the pact between Faust and Mephistopheles in exchange for the world, and a Pelagian impulse, as Augustine interprets it, to assume exclusive management of one's own destiny.

In these one-sided partnerships, God is often treated as a bottled genie, catering to the activist's will. Recall the notorious rationale offered some clergymen by President McKinley for annexing the Philippines: "I went on my knees and prayed to Almighty God for light and guidance more than one night. And one night it came to me this way —that there was nothing left for us to do but take them all, and educate the Filipinos, and uplift and civilize and Christianize them, and by God's grace do the very best we could by them, as our fellowmen for whom Christ also died. And then I went to bed and went to sleep and slept soundly."

An amusing parody of the same attitude shows up in preacher invocations at games and sport banquets: "O Great Referee of the sky, we come before you this evening to seek your blessing! Let the wings of your angels play at the right and left of our teammates. Be the divine center on our team, give us victory in the game of life, reserve us a permanent seat in your heavenly coliseum!" The words are directed to the God of War, whose hosannas often tune down after a succession of losing seasons. To most critics, these prayers read like half-aware projections of one's own immaturity—an idolatrous grab for power, the will to win at all costs.

Even Theravada Buddhists with their strict apophatic prayer tradition have proved susceptible to this distortion of the will. In two Paganese inscriptions from an eleventh century tomb, you will find two differing prayers—the first by Queen Amana, the second by Queen Caw. The first is a selfless bodhisattva petition. Amana asks that her own karmic merit be showered upon the king, her subjects, and even Yama, lord of the dead. "I pray to cross samsara full of the good graces—modest in my wants, even-tempered, compassionate, wise, conscious of causes, large-handed, unforgetful, and affectionate." Yet in utter contrast, Queen Caw prays, not for a spiritual nirvana, but just a better rebirth into her present egocentric universe: "Before I reach nirvana, by virtue of the meritorious works I have achieved on such a big scale, I wish virtue and prosperity if born again as a human being. If I am born a spirit, I wish to be beautiful, sweet-voiced, well-proportioned in limbs, the beloved and honored darling of every human being and spirit. May I have lots of gold, silver, rubies, coral, pearls. Wherever I am born, may I not know one speck of misery. And after I have tasted and enjoyed the happiness of human beings and spirits, may I at last attain the peaceful bliss of nirvana."[3]

The flimsy supports for any self-calculating faith often stand exposed in those wounded by unfamiliar defeat. I remember a woman whose boyfriend fled without a hint of their impending break-up. Her snapback reaction was first to depose and then deny God in retaliation, an anger that swept away everything in the cosmos. Feeling deeply for her, and also offering to share my own faith, I suggested that God could understand this angry loss, and also her resentment, too. But she went on to describe the only God she knew—a figure of comfort and success, indistinguishable from her own willful construction of the world, someone ministering just to her needs. There was no room for the sharp edges of reality, ready to prune away self-centered wishes. She seemed unable or unwilling to mature beyond this Velveteen Rabbit image of the sacred.

The Bible itself often appears to endorse this manipulative frame of mind, mostly by offering unconditional guarantees that God will answer any heartfelt prayer. According to the early Deuteronomist interpretation of religious history, Yahweh, pressured by Israel's prayers, let her win battles when she obeyed him, and lose battles when she sinned. Yet eventually Israel discovered from the long humiliating experience of loss that often devout people fail, while the wicked flourish. Also during their Babylonian Exile, Jews learned from new direct friendships with their Gentile neighbors that non-Jews, too, perhaps believed in the same God. Thus, one providential effect of all their apparently undeserved suffering might be a broader vision of God's concern for the entire human race, a theme rendered admirably in the Book of Jonah.

For Reinhold Niebuhr, the will to win, the Nietzschean or Adlerian will to power, serves as the psychological counterpart to what Christians call original sin. As explained before, the religious factor should always be treated as dialectical. Thus, humility toward the sacred at the same time includes self-assertion on behalf of the sacred. As the child grows progressively aware of life, a puny ego confronting an immense universe, how can the will to live be separated from the will to power? You yearn to expand, to give your life a meaning beyond yourself. Fear may lead to courage, but each effort to consolidate what you have gained may justify new fears. Your very security requires an extension of power. And each tactic of self-defense easily turns into a tactic of aggression.[4]

Martin Luther King, Jr. has popularized Niebuhr's teaching in his sermon on the Drum Major Instinct, preached at Ebenezer Baptist Church a few months before his assassination. The urge to be ahead, to achieve honor and reputation, a creditable ingredient in its own way, can be turned against people, not just by advertisers peddling a whiskey for persons of distinction, or a flashy car for the envy of neighbors. In a more devious way, it prompts snobbish churches to boast of high incomes and doctorates among their clientele. It also motivates the worst racists, stripped down to their last shreds of self-esteem, the pride of mere skin pigmentation. Instead of materialistic success, King asks his followers to achieve loving service, like Christ, transforming their enforced legacy as servants into a free vocation to serve.[5]

Selling the Good News

An utter subversion of King's ideal can be found in the so-called prosperity gospel of some current televangelists. It is difficult to cite its proponents with dispassionate accuracy, mostly because of all their P. T. Barnum hype. However, a few themes recur. Like Christian Science and other traditions that William James calls "healthy-minded," these preachers claim poverty or sickness are not really God's plan, but just an individual's own faithless perception. Faith means positive-thinking, the best way to befriend a God who has guaranteed success to his favorite children.

The more money you send God through a particular TV pulpit, the greater material dividends God will return on your investment. You must state your claim on him boldly, telling him what his part in the Covenant ought to be. One of Kenneth Copeland's best-sellers is *The Laws of Prosperity*. His wife Gloria has entitled her book *God's Will Is Prosperity*. Terry Cole-Whittaker in her book *How to Have More in a Have-Not World* promises "you can have exactly what you want, when you want it, all the time. You don't need to take a vow of poverty to achieve spirituality. Affluence is your right." For twenty-five dollars—the price at least a few years ago—her weekly TV program in San Diego could enhance your awareness of abundance by mailing from the Science of Mind Church International a "prosperity kit," consisting of cassette tape, booklet, and bumper sticker.[6]

Only a few privileged cultures and eras could foster this mercenary style or find it palatable. It seems packaged for the upwardly mobile in a capitalist society where wealth and success are live possibilities, insulated from serious misery elsewhere. At worst, it panders to the conquerors, but not the defeated, except to depress or narcotize them further by prompting infantile, misdirected hopes. Friendship with God is reduced mostly to an insurance policy, with little genuine trust and risk. The prototypes of this counterfeit are Luther's villain Tetzel, or Chaucer's Pardoner, both hucksters of gimcrack religious shortcuts.

To be fair, I concede that the average electronic church may launch its history with sterling motives, broadcasting a spiritual mission. But the huge expenses of weekly production demand an increasingly wider base of audience appeal, and then a more militant campaign to raise money from the audience. So the religious message tends to become more commercial and thus theatrical. The medium shapes the message, or more accurately, the TV program begins to exist mostly for its own self-propagation. This same misplaced emphasis pervades many door-to-door evangelists, concerned less with the vital implications of their religious message, than the sheer act of getting out there and preaching it. Too many seem obsessed by communication skills and gadgets of the hard sell, as if the truth of their message can be vindicated by its very dissemination.

In other words, some activists are so immersed in the sales process that they expect to assure their own salvation by toting up consumer converts. For instance, in Japan the Nichiren Buddhist *Shakubuku Kyoten*—literally, the manual for destruction and conquest—has promised karmic merit and leadership positions to those with the largest number of converts. My own theology department was the target for a similar conversion policy some years ago, when a nervous middle-aged stranger knocked at the office door. She claimed to need assistance in locating an obscure anecdote from the Book of Judges. But as she watched me reach for a Bible to refresh my memory, her earnest quest suddenly dissolved into a shabby sales trick. Announcing herself an Assembly of God missionary, she left me with two abrasive messages: Catholic priests do not know their Bible. And anyone not born-again, in the manner approved by her particular Church, is destined for hell. Eager to exit immediately after tossing this grenade, she gave the impression of a wind-up doll with a recorded message.

Trying to cool down over the intrusion, and hoping to salvage something of worth from her visit, I urged the woman to repeat her message slower, so that we could both listen to its full import. Then I sought clarification of a few terms employed. I inquired whether she herself believed each assertion as explained, where she had been taught this exact formulation, and what comfort or embarrassment she experienced in performing an errand like this. She disclosed a certainty that her own salvation depended on delivering this message intact, regardless of my accepting or even understanding it. I then joked about my corresponding concern for her salvation, too, especially since her mission might be disqualified by garbled presentation to a tough customer like myself. Smiling at this unlikely consequence, she claimed to feel at peace, now her errand had been accomplished. So like an anonymous hired courier, she had hoped to drop off the package unexamined, without being pressed to assume mature responsibility for its contents.

Religious Paranoia

Thus, winning at all costs may decline just to rivalry or argument for its own sake, and the strenuous will to believe may prove itself no more than the will to make-believe. Once the illusion of control is endangered, panic and anxiety usually ensue, forecasting a siege of religious paranoia.

If trapped in a paranoid situation, you tend to feel humiliated or betrayed by everyone. Yet rather than retreat before this disappointment, you might counterattack, hoping to avoid any surprise attack by anticipating it. Yet this is not the alertness of a clever hunter, but a tired policeman under stress, apt to shoot at shadows. The enemy lurks everywhere, poisoning the water supply by fluoridation, polluting racial purity, undermining the nation's moral stamina. To compensate for this fear, some people turn rigidly arrogant, with pretensions of control and competence. Litigious, hypersensitive to any slights, they tend to view others as either the instigators or the victims of manipulative power relationships. And uncertain of their own autonomy, perhaps they grovel before authority figures, or on the contrary, bristle at any hint of outside control or intrusion.[7]

This description suggests a potential strain of paranoia running through some familiar religious stereotypes. Conjuring up the typical authoritarian religious personality, you first picture inquisitors, censors, and doctrinal purists from the right wing of all religious movements, especially in the Catholic tradition, as immortalized by lurid gothic novels. Often repressing or belittling their own religious experience, figures of this sort are prone to treat the mystic or prophet with suspicion. But the same paranoid disposition, prompting a Church autocrat to fret about orthodoxy, may foster in others an attitude of excessive docility or rebellion.

Though prevalent in totalitarian societies, the paranoid mode also flourishes in the United States—our largest inner cities threatened by youth gang wars, our citizens more and more litigious, our political campaigns marred by defamation and resentment. The milieu of capitalist economies is Hobbesian, with price wars, combative takeovers, stock-market lotteries, and multinationals ruled by anonymous agents. Sun Tzu's *Art of War,* written in 500 B.C.E., has won a current readership in Japan and western Europe. Applied to business, his tactics demand a thorough information network of double agents to smoke out the competitor's weak points and take advantage. You might pretend to cooperate fully or in part, for example, or decide when to buy out a rival, or change a marketing mix to avoid direct confrontation.[8]

An aura of the competitive, suspicious, and vindictive clings to many religious groups and institutions, especially those brooding over their own history as a once persecuted minority. The most tragic example of this in recent memory is the final address by Jim Jones to his dying flock at Jonestown. Groping to legitimize mass suicide, he was preaching spiritual warfare against the world, the need for endless vigilance and distrust. Again, just a few years ago, trucks laden with disaster provisions converged toward mountain crypts in southern Montana near a ranch of three thousand acres, site of the Church Universal and Triumphant. Declaring this era a dark cycle between the Age of Pisces and the New Age of Aquarius, the Church's New Age leader Elizabeth Clare Prophet predicted an inevitable nuclear war with the Soviet Union. Even today the underground chambers are fully equipped bomb shelters, called the Heart of the Inner Retreat, where followers huddling for the apocalypse live out a siege spirituality.

Many religious movements seem to invite persecution, as a deliberate or unconscious rationale. Wars of the Spirit give them recognition and a distinctive identity, much like a nation confirming its solidarity by opposition to some common external enemy. For example, recall the provocative martyr-mystique that surrounds much of early Mormon history. Just as St. Paul found glory in being persecuted, so Joseph Smith would claim he felt like a fish out of water if he were to lack persecutors. Brigham Young admonished young missionaries departing from Utah that they must not preach about "the beauty of their mountain home, but dwell on the idea of persecution, and call the poor into a persecuted church." In another religious tradition, the contentious thirteenth century Buddhist Nichiren, denouncing a succession of rulers and priests, admits he is the most intractable man in Japan. The gospel of Nichiren offers this provocation: become either his convert, or else his enemy and persecutor.[9]

Political harassment and martyrdom have pervaded the heritage of every Jew, the early Christians, and many Protestant sectarians fleeing religious wars in Europe. And these wounds have often left a sour, unforgiving legacy. In my own experience, no matter how much I learn about the fiery Semitic temperament, or antithetic patterns in Hebrew rhetoric, I cannot pray specific lines of the Hebrew Psalms: "Lord, I love you, but I hate your foes," or "Protect me, but dash out the brains of my enemy's children!" Furthermore, if I had shared in ancient Christian deliberations on selecting the New Testament canon, I would have cast a minority vote to exclude the Book of Revelation. Even Calvin could argue in hindsight for its omission. It has become an armory of proof-texts for endless paranoid and obsessive misinterpretations.

The Armageddon Mentality

Based on scattered images, numbers, and slogans from Revelation and the Book of Daniel, an Armageddon war scenario still transfixes the minds of many Evangelical Christians. "I think a war with the Soviet Union is inevitable, if I read Bible prophecy properly," televangelist Pat Robertson told his presidential campaign audiences in the 1988 Primaries. "The chances are that the U.S. will come in as a defender of Israel." The world is so corrupt, he reasoned, that God cannot do anything except destroy it, and build Christ's new kingdom in its place. When Robertson forces later won the early delegate election in Michigan, their candidate at once proclaimed, "The Christians have won. What a breakthrough for the Kingdom!" Thus, colored by delusions of self-reference, one's own political rivals begin to look like the enemies of God. I do not think voters disputed this candidate's right to believe and preach an apocalyptic scenario. But many feared its potential as a dogmatic self-fulfilling guide to foreign policy.[10]

An ironic parallel to Robertson's militant dualism can be found at the earliest roots of American history. Columbus himself read his Bible from a similar millennarian perspective. He persuaded royal patrons to accept his own literal interpretation of Matthew 24:14: "And this gospel of the Kingdom will be proclaimed throughout the earth as a testimony to all nations; and then the end will come." Columbus argued that the conquest and conversion of this new continent would be the semi-final events leading to a destruction of the Anti-Christ and the known world.[11] This lordly little sailor expected to inaugurate a new heaven and a new earth.

The dualistic imagination, introduced in chapter 3, attempts to carve dichotomies between superego and id, God and Satan, heavenly purity and a corruptible world. Climaxed by President Ronald Reagan's designation of the Soviet Union as the "Evil Empire," America for at least a half century has been defining itself and its policies in these exaggerated polarities. With current abatement of the Cold War fervor, many bewildered dualists are now rummaging for some new externalized Satan—Latin drug czars, Arab terrorists, Japanese cartels, or abstractions like illiteracy, unemployment, even political correctness.

Preoccupied with locating an external enemy of this sort, the average Armageddon Christian is reluctant to tolerate just a neutral, or a friendly but divergent viewpoint. For example, the director of the Carolina Conservative Coalition tried to explain his own beliefs about Armageddon to an interviewer during the 1988 Republican primaries. Distraught by the irreconcilable conflict between good and evil spirits, he chanced on an incredible illustration. As a physician himself, this man could not help but admire the skill of one particular colleague, a heart specialist for children, who spends long hours in the operating room, and often waives fees for poor patients. "People love him," the physician said. "But the sucker's a nonbeliever. I've talked to him about it. He just won't accept Christ." Satan must have engineered this man's success in order to convince people that "someone who isn't a Christian can be successful. Satan is tricky that way. But in the end, that poor sucker is going to hell because he's not born-again."[12]

A favorite catchword for Armageddon militants is the biblical verse, "those not with us are against us." And a xenophobic motto, long prevalent and unquestioned in Christian history, claims *extra ecclesiam nulla salus*—there is no salvation outside the Church. Viewed mostly as an enemy, then, the religious outsider becomes someone to be converted forcefully or bracketed out of one's life, and devalued as a human being. Here the Christ who loves and forgives his enemies seems to have vanished from consciousness. Yet even in combat, the Taoist and Zen Buddhist martial arts train you to view an opponent as the mirror image of yourself, not as a person to hate or fear. And Gandhi, attacking corrupt systems but not people, insists you respect and trust your opponents, giving them credit for the same honest faith as yourself. "Just as no human being is so bad as to be beyond redemption," he concludes, echoing Niebuhr's remarks on the ambiguity of power, "no human being is so perfect as to warrant destroying someone wrongly considered to be wholly evil."

Religious Obsession

Religious self-assertion, foremost among the activist distortions mentioned above, results in a one-sided partnership with the personal God. Now in the obsessive temperament, this partnership is unbalanced in the opposite direction, tilting toward God as the ultimate scorekeeper and warden, ever demanding more of you. One major side-effect of excessive activism can be cited immediately, the *karoshi* disorder. This is a recent term devised by Japanese news columnists, registering the fall-out from their economic miracle—death from the stress of overwork. Employee overtime has too often become the single way to gauge corporate loyalty.

In a parallel manner the spiritual workaholic gives too much weight to performance ratings. The subordinate in this lopsided relationship is often someone left insecure from an earlier loss of love or protection, but now hankering for success as an act of self-vindication. A fiercely busy pastor and social worker, for example, once disclosed to me his well-concealed depression. He would have killed himself long before this, had it not been for his clients who needed him, the people whom his death would disappoint or unhinge. God never seemed satisfied, no matter how many souls were rescued for heaven. Consistent with this warped spirituality, the poor man labored desperately each day just to stay alive. Like some haunted Christ-figure in a Graham Greene novel, by bringing others peace, even through his own self-destruction, he hoped himself to find peace.

This description suggests the characteristic traits of an obsessive-compulsive disorder. A person of this temperament relishes the activist vocabulary of purpose, decision, and moral earnestness. But a driven, rigid nuance has to be added to each word. Reluctant to let go of a decision once made, you can be expected to redo or undo, to touch up or perfect. Or you become absorbed by an infinite number of preliminaries so that the awesome climax of deciding never arrives. Distrustful of whims, hunches, and any impetuous gesture, you want a sense of resolute effort to characterize every action. Insecure about your own autonomy, you usually ask for detailed external directives.

The religious domain offers an obsessive person unlimited scope for doubt and guilt, two problems central to the case-load of any spiritual counselor. These two disorders will now be examined, especially the distinction between genuine guilt and its destructive counterfeits.

The Doubting Madness

The French call an obsessive-compulsive disorder *folie de doute* or the doubting madness. Routine religious doubts, of course, often surface in an atmosphere of disquiet and guilt because people have been taught by some religious traditions to repress them as a mark of infidelity or satanic temptation. It is unfortunate that the average religious shepherd and flock often lock themselves in a conspiracy of mutual polite deception—each concealing doubts from the other, reluctant to shock or disappoint. Yet the presence of genuine doubt, on the contrary, may show promise of a faith beginning to awake, independent and self-critical.

The habit of doubting has other explanations, too. Perhaps your mind has been conditioned to expect Cartesian mathematical certainty in a single empirical field of knowledge. You may then try to transfer this limited criterion of truth to wider personal or metaphysical ranges of experience. Questions like the following can stun an intellect accustomed to rudimentary problem-solving: do your parents love you, can you trust anyone, does God exist, do you yourself actually exist, how can you know that you really know?

However, the obsessive doubt has a quality lacking in ordinary doubt. Driven by parental or group imperatives, disowning most of your own genuine feelings and convictions, you might never affirm, deny, or choose anything wholeheartedly. Thus, you may flee to the shelter of dogma, regulations, a rigidly structured religious community, just to avoid the harassments of doubt. An earnest recovering addict often cites motives like these for choosing a strict religious sect or cult as an authoritarian half-way house. A famous poet once praised her new-found Catholic faith precisely because it gave her moral life the secure discipline of a sonnet structure. She could not handle the chaotic self-indulgence of free verse.

A focus on sheer literal detail, preventing things from being seen in actual perspective, may predispose a person to feel too certain one moment, too uncertain the next. What others think a minor detail can suddenly change the entire picture for an obsessive consciousness. As psychologist David Shapiro wisely observes, both doubt and dogma may be defenses against the more direct, spontaneous experience of conviction.[13]

Thus, by submitting to the burdensome rituals, one may hope to reach God, with all worries and doubts trimmed away. Often the aim is not to seek truth, but to follow a secure path blindly, whether it proves true or false. This attitude characterizes many so-called true believers, who seal off their faith from all possible criticism. For these people commonly fear infidelity and damnation more than a little self-deceit. As an illustration of this frame of mind, recall Dostoevsky's passionate credo, written in prison: "If anyone proved to me that Christ was outside the Truth, and it really meant that Truth was outside Christ, then I should prefer to remain with Christ than with Truth."

Counterfeits of Guilt

In his studies on obsessive religious behavior, Freud traces neurotic guilt feelings back to the violation of an individual's private taboos or ceremonial defenses. It is essential to clarify a few terms here. As defined in chapter 1, conscience is a sense of moral accountability toward the sacred center of one's life. Thus, conscience must be distinguished from the Freudian superego, that undifferentiated legacy of social and family values communicated to each individual. In a maturing conscience, each of us must gradually test out, select or discard, and personalize this superego legacy. Genuine guilt results from a deliberate violation of one's conscience, whereas irrational guilt feelings or counterfeit guilt arise from a conscious or even unconscious violation of the superego.

Like most priest-confessors, I have spent years hearing out anonymous voices in the confessional and helping them recognize some crucial distinctions. The qualitative difference between the irrational guilt feelings Freud describes and a genuine mature guilt, between the unexamined superego heritage and one's own examined conscience, between rebellion against a sheer external directive and against an authentic inner directive. I have always considered it the mark of an integrated human being to take responsibility for one's own unique appropriated values, for any conscious betrayal of these values, and for the possibility of genuine contrition and restitution. "If only people could realize," says Jung, "what an enrichment it is to find one's own guilt, what a sense of honor and spiritual dignity!"

According to a crucial axiom in my own pastoral training, any sin chosen for sacramental confession must be viewed as just a limited symbol of profound inarticulate guilt. And any instant of absolution by a priest must be the limited symbol, too, of God's more pervasive forgiveness, not blowing hot and cold to match each variation in one's own unsteady moral life. Thus, it would be wiser to focus, not on a computer inventory of sinful acts, but on patterns of habitual sinfulness or guilt.

In the classical approach to scrupulous or obsessive penitents, the priest confessor had once been expected to shoulder their burden of conscience and order them under religious obedience to curtail excessive worries, prayers, and ceremonials. However, in the last half-century most priests have been taught to treat each obsessive confession as a problem more emotional than moral. Except for sickbed emergency interviews, I was cautioned in my own training never to fall back on the old authoritarian strategy. This discredited approach could induce worse suffering and regression, or might play into a parental authority complex at the root of these obsessions. After helping the individual distinguish between a sin and an emotional disorder, the priest confessor should then recommend psychological counseling. If equipped to offer it oneself, the priest should try to meet a client in some neutral non-confessional setting, dissociated from overtones of sin and judgment.[14]

It would be otiose—and obsessive—to document typical obsessive cases in confessional or clinical settings. Some chronic victims give the impression that instinctual nesting or hoarding messages in the brain have gone awry, twitching and spinning aimlessly. And thus, prayers must be repeated, hands scrubbed raw, faith doubted and reaffirmed.

Such rituals have become ends in themselves, and the stated religious or secular rationale for doing them can only be secondary. In many of these narrowed, driven lives, however, a few patterns recur.

The first can be illustrated in the adolescent experiences of Fern from *The Divorce Sonnets,* a novel by Harry Taylor.[15] Once quite devoted in her visits to a local Catholic church, and even toying with hopes to become a nun, Fern always associates that earlier stage of her life with spiritual hardships—cold baths, frigid winter morning Masses, intricate penances. But one day at college a terrible incident occurs. While praying near the altar rail, she imagines a prominent phallus on the crucifix figure. With effort she wipes this shocking image from her mind, but it returns again whenever she enters a church to pray. Although this obsessive period ceases, she never completely recovers, and stops going to church altogether.

Freud recounts similar episodes in his famous Rat Man and Wolf Man cases. Whenever the Rat Man would say "May God protect her" in prayers for his fiancée, a hostile "not" would suddenly dart out of his unconscious mind and insert itself into the formula, which he felt compelled to shorten or paraphrase the next time he tried to pray. During early adolescence the Wolf Man's prayers were interrupted by such blasphemous word associations as "God-swine" or "God-dung," and he would think of the Trinity whenever he saw three heaps of horse manure on the road. In a comparable dilemma, the young Luther, driven to endless confessions, penances, and tortuous exactitude about rubrics for Mass, managed by his public deterioration unconsciously to caricature and attack the rules themselves.

As a teacher, I am familiar with this same curious ambiguity in the student who tries too earnestly to carry out format details in some assigned term paper. Persistent questions about its exact length, spacing, and margins suggest cumulatively that the specifications themselves must be cruelly arbitrary. In all these parallel situations, you perceive a riotous ambivalence—love compromised by hate, faith by doubt, the moment of decision nibbled away by hesitation, dissent in the very gesture of pious obedience. What devout people often externalize as "temptations" from God or Satan are, from another perspective, simply their own flickering ambivalence.

Another aspect of obsessive temperaments, noted shrewdly by Freud, is the maneuver of displaced guilt feelings. He mentions a government official, almost amoral in his repeated molestation of young girls, but fastidious in washing and ironing the florin notes he uses to pay Freud for his therapy because money might transmit germs. One of my clients once described his odd rituals after each evening of mutual masturbation with his girl friend. Next day he would spend hours scrubbing the sofa, his clothing, anything else he may have touched, fretting that a remnant sperm might impregnate some innocent woman later seated there. I knew of his strict moral values from earlier therapy sessions. By ritual diversions, he was probably trying to avoid facing his direct transgression of these values. The cleaning seemed an unconscious attempt at self-purification, too, possibly a gesture of religious penitence, though he had never looked at it that way.

In a similar displacement, many pious obsessive people express a disproportionate sense of guilt over distracted prayers or minuscule flaws in carrying out ritual prescriptions. But they seem perfunctory about more serious duties of family or social justice. This counterfeit style of prayer and ritual surely deserves prophetic denunciation. For it seems staged to distract God from noticing the neglect of really important values. On the other hand, you can feel empathy for this awkward groping, in even the crudest symbols of displacement, to express and come to terms with an otherwise unmanageable guilt.

All three of the activist religious disorders examined in this chapter share a common deviation. They are swept off balance by an ideal of absolute religious purity. Self-assertive personalities tend to identify this flawless cause with their own will, the paranoid are convinced that at least all other causes are impure, and obsessive people refrain from action because no cause is pure enough. Yet this unwavering fixation on the ideal is challenged expressly by Emmanuel Mounier, whose philosophy of personalism tried to bridge the worlds of existentialism, Marxism, and Christian spirituality. For him, the worst activist heresy is a lofty self-envelopment, refraining from engagement until the cause is pure, with no risk of dirty hands.

The best spiritual activism, Mounier believes, demands bravery in the service of love, based not on obstinacy or bravado, but on a relaxed trust in God. It cannot function without self-criticism and a balanced sense of reality. "The creative force of self-commitment," he concludes, "is born of tensions it excites between the imperfection of the cause, and its own absolute fidelity to the values implicated." This disparity should protect you from fanaticism, in a state of vigilant criticism. The risk and partial obscurity surrounding every decision keeps you insecure but resilient—the psychological climate for all heroic action.[16]

6

Way of Affectivity

Both preceding chapters reasserted that activism, affectivity, and contemplation must all pervade each sacred Way. For the single-minded development of just one component leads to distortion.

It is easy to imagine the Way of Action thrown off balance, for instance, once a loving interest in people has faded. The energetic Miss Quested in Forster's *Passage to India* apologizes at last to Aziz, whom she has mistakenly blamed and ruined. But her apology miscarries, for it rests only on honesty and cold justice. "She had felt, while she recanted, no passion of love for those whom she had wronged. Truth is not truth in that exacting land unless there go with it kindness and more kindness and kindness again."[1]

Some gospel activists, as remarked before, blunder by sizing you up as just a prospective convert, or by seeming to serve the God in you, but not the you. In a similar manner, eager to conquer illness, one doctor may be too busy with symptoms, research, calculation of risks, the tactics of intervention, a routine of brisk professional hospital visits. Another doctor, no less trained and informed, spending time with each patient, listening to each unique story, seems to treat the ill person rather than just another illness.

The indispensable ingredient in these examples is love, which constitutes a distinctive spirituality of its own, the Way of Affectivity. Love here means not just God's love, or the cosmic life-force of Eros, but most of all the ordinary closeness and affection between two friends or lovers.

True love is easily underestimated. Folk wisdom claims love is blind. On the contrary, what blinds you is infatuation on one hand, but also detached objectivity on the other. For love stands at the midpoint between spatial extremes of engulfment and remoteness. Genuine love, says philosopher Max Scheler, opens your spiritual eyes to ever higher values in the loved one. For example, the unique endowments in a man's fiancée, neglected by the distant observer, are discernible only to the sharper eye of love. Knowing her may increase his love for her. But without a prior readiness to love this unique woman, he may underestimate or not even perceive her at all.

Mature affectivity, then, is not blind, nor is it sentimental and overly dependent. To expect too much is softness that ends in bitterness, novelist Flannery O'Connor observes, for real charity is hard and endures. This bond between two lovers is a pledge to anticipate and nourish the ideal potential in both individuals. Neither of you, therefore, can be defined as just a support or appendage to the other. As true lovers, you each share fully in the identity of the other, without losing your own unique identity. In fact, your commitment to the growth of each other may at times call for "tough love," a prophetic reprimand or momentary clash.

Taking its cue from the framework of chapter 5, the present study begins by identifying the god-image and mature response common to a spirituality of affectivity. Potential imbalances in this Way will soon surface, notably an excessive dependency and self-abandonment.

The God of Love

You will recall the god-image familiar to most activists in every religious tradition—an indispensable partner in saving the world, or co-creating an ideal society. The Way of Affectivity, however, now shifts emphasis from both task and partnership, and begins to appreciate the living identity of this colleague. A keen Hindu recognition of this transition from activism to love can be found in the Bhagavad Gita. Arjuna despairs of his own efforts to live out the conflicting Activist Way and Contemplative Way. Yet appreciating the limitations of both these two Ways, his charioteer, the god Krishna, urges him to adopt a third option, the Way of Affectivity. "Set your heart on me alone," he advises. "Take refuge in devotion to me, and surrender to me the fruit of all your work" (12: 8, 11).

As so many mystics explain it, God takes an endless initiative in loving us. God yearns to be as near as Krishna to Radha, Rama to Sita, or the Tibetan yab and yum deities in candid sexual embrace. Kabir, the great Bengali poet claimed by both Muslims and Hindus, sings of his unrelieved passion for God, uttering the name of his beloved in a frenzy all day long, seeing nothing anywhere but God. "He is the only adorable one to me. I have no other love." God is as close to Kabir as a bee to the wind supporting it, a lyre to its player, a lotus to the water's surface, a river to the ocean into which it pours.

God waits for Theresa of Avila at the central room in her soul—a kernel hidden beneath several tough layers of Spanish palmito leaves, each of which must be successively pealed away to reach the treasure. Attar of Neishapur, a Sufi mystic, portrays this long desired union in a graphic parable. Knocking at the door, a lover first announces, "It's I," and is turned away. But after long meditation on this rejection, there is a second attempt to knock. "Who is it?" asks a voice beyond the door. And the one knocking now responds, "It's you." At this word the door opens.

To match this personal God, the spontaneous response can only be love for love. To befriend God, of course, can mean all the tenderness, candor, and mutual challenge that mark your mature relationships with other friends. But the classical mystics fix their gaze mostly on the rapturous embrace itself. They imagine an exchange of marital vows, or even of both hearts. Francis of Assisi identifies with the sufferings of Christ to such an extent that his palms and feet are marked with the stigmata. Donning a sacred mask, an African or Balinese dancer searches meditatively for the god or ancestral spirit present there. And God is summoned to take possession of the individual. The Indian mystic Ramakrishna, eager to befriend God as closely as Rama's monkey servant Hanuman, spends months perching in the trees, eating only roots and fruit, and with part of his loincloth dragging like a tail, hopping instead of walking. Or cuddling a statue of the child Rama, he dances with it, and gives it piggyback rides.

Beyond a certain measure, playful endearments like those of Ramakrishna, lavished on keepsakes and facsimiles of the beloved, can lapse into idolatry. In her story "The Widow," Jhabvala traces this spiritual decline most vividly. Durga is left a widow by her rich husband, who has made cunning arrangements for her financial independence. Though her relatives soon begin to prey on Durga, she is able to outsmart each of their ambushes. But an elderly aunt discovers the right formula to bring her down. Bhuaji awakens Durga's interest in the god Krishna as someone likely to sit and have tea with the widow in her living room. He is now a baby to bathe and tuck into bed with a kiss, now a lover with whom Durga can lie at night in her husband's bed. The widow's lonely existence gradually surrenders to these fantasies. Beginning to talk with Krishna statues in her home, she yearns for them to come alive and make love to her.

Durga soon becomes obsessed with a self-centered adolescent tenant upstairs, whom she mistakes for the handsome Krishna. Yet when one desperate appeal after another fails to touch this boy, she loses the will to resist her predators. Unbathed in an old crumpled sari, her hair undone, she at last dumps out all her jewels and money on the floor. Buaji stands at her side, murmuring in ironic approval, "Only if we give up everything, will God come to us."[2]

This love-sick piety is open to the most flamboyant distortions. Similar to the Hindu Bhakti Way, popular Catholic piety in many cultures often centers on plaster madonnas to be kissed and stroked, or crucifixes that shed purportedly real tears and blood. Commenting on his Puerto Rican Catholic childhood, the boxer José Torres describes his young companion's father, who once cursed and slapped a large crucifix on the wall. This man could not endure the Jesus figure hanging there inert, letting the boy make so many idiotic spelling mistakes. I recall no less disturbing a scene in my own childhood, when a seven-year-old Polish-American friend was being scolded by her mother. The woman snatched a crucifix to spit on it, insisting this was how her daughter's misbehavior hurt Jesus. To repair the injury done her mother, the little girl began to cry, and then ran over to cradle the image, as if it were an injured rag doll.

If religious antics like these offend my own Catholic taste, they must be intolerable to the aniconic temperament of Jews, Muslims, and Cromwell's Puritans. Yet as observed in chapter 3, most world traditions make room for at least two distinctive religious preferences. Based on differences in culture and temperament, people will treat human images as either an aid or hindrance to communion with the sacred.

A more balanced display of loving service can be illustrated in the daily rites of a brahmin family I once visited in Madras. Though less florid than those described above, their puja devotions were very concrete and dramatic. Removing a favorite statue of Krishna from its tabernacle, the head of the family proceeded to welcome, comfort, bathe, clothe, and feed the image. Yet these informed Hindus seemed careful to frame their ceremony with explicit prayers of invocation and dismissal. By separating the rite from ordinary time and space, they indicated that the sacred does not come and go, but our images and projections do. Perhaps the best rationale for puja of this sort is the philosopher Shankara's famous prayer excusing our finite imagination. He apologizes for trying to visualize the formless Brahman, for praising in hymns the ineffable Brahman, for visiting in shrines the omnipresent Brahman.

Religious Dependency

This book so far has singled out three different seductive idols—the sheer words of a text, one's own will and its activist agenda, and now, a cherished image or live human being. What is true of Durga in the story above is also exemplified by Elizabeth from the earlier Jhabvala story recounted in chapter 4. Both Durga's young tenant and Elizabeth's husband Raju are bound to disappoint these women, for no mortal can match the divine lover both women need and claim. Elizabeth, we recall, had developed a submissive personality, steering away from conflict with Margaret and Raju at all costs. Ready to sacrifice her own desires and identity, she wanted only to merge into her husband's career, opinions, and sheltering love. The infatuations of Elizabeth and also of Durga seem omens of a far more pervasive dependency.

Idolatry involves two basic misunderstandings. In the religious search, perhaps you may stop short at pyramid crystals, the presence of some psychic, a particular yoga or ecological scheme, and mistake mere rest stops for the sacred summit. Second, and more important, by worshiping sexuality, fame, intellectual or even spiritual ability, you subordinate your entire humanity to some diminished shadow-image of yourself. And these projections become especially addictive and enslaving when they are focused on another human being. "Deflation of the over-invested partner, parent, or friend is a creative act," sociologist Ernest Becker cautions. Without this deflation, you cannot reaffirm your own "inner freedom of growth that transcends the particular object and is not bound to it.[3]

The Affective Way approaches God as an ideal friend or spouse, but also as a loving mother or father. "Can a mother forget the child of her womb?" asks the Book of Isaiah. "Even if she forgets, still I will not forget you" (49:15). This parental image implies a protected, dependent sort of relationship, which at best will expand into a balanced interdependence on God, an attitude explored at the beginning of chapter 5. Most imbalances in the Affective Way are commonly traceable to an earlier developmental period, when a child's urge to be loved is frustrated, or at the other extreme, indulged to the point of fixation.

Childlike Interdependence

Most people forget the prolonged vulnerability of their earliest years. In comparison with other species, human beings face a longer period of physical and psychological dependency after leaving the womb. We are born so helpless, that some biologists refer to our first years as the final stage of fetal life. Lacking the instinctual equipment for self-preservation, we have to lean on others for nourishment, protection, and constant encouraging lessons about how to love and be lovable. Clambering up to adulthood as the elusive pinnacle of autonomy and control, most of us dread the probable descent to relative dependency again, economic and physical. In the final moments of life, every mortal must learn once again to receive and not just to give.[4]

As the wisest training for mature interdependence, a child needs to feel so secure within a circle of familiar toys and love, that any ventures away from this haven become endurable. It ought to be possible for miniature heroes and heroines to crawl toward boundaries and beyond, engage all their dragons, and turn back anytime for reassurance. Thus, the maturing individual can master a middle ground between excessive autonomy and clinging.

One remarkable child who survived this earliest crisis of trusting dependence is Martin Luther. As psychologist Erik Erikson conjectures, the boy's mother must have provided her son with his earliest source of trust, "that original optimism, the assumption that somebody is there, without which we cannot live." Later as a monk, broken by the strain to win God's affection and approval, Luther turned back to his childhood trust as the model for a recovered trust in God. Justification had to come from faith alone, he realized, and from God's favor alone. This affirmation of sound ultimate dependence could free his heart from the constant anxiety of having to prove himself before anyone else.[5]

"I want to depend, but nobody lets me. For the past six months or so, I've been wishing I had someone to act as a mother to me. Someone I could confide in, someone who'd take decisions out of my hands." This complaint by a Japanese male law student, a familiar pattern in the therapy practice of Takeo Doi, suggests that the criteria for a balanced dependence may be culturally relative. Whereas Europe and America idealize the lone independent hero, traditional Japanese society, especially in child-rearing and its vertical business relationships, has mostly preferred heroes more dependent and filial.

The Japanese verb *amaeru,* lacking an English equivalent, connotes a need to be loved and indulged, to feel at home in one's surroundings, to snuggle up to someone, to hanker for the lost mother-child envelopment. Doi even identifies the Shinto heaven as a realm that includes the emperor, nation, ancestors, and land, all "beyond the anguish of unsatisfied *amae.*" Offering an explanation similar to this, psychologist Margaret Mahler in her object-relations theory describes the culmination of our human life cycle as "symbiotic fusion with the all-good mother, who was at one time part of the self in a blissful state of well-being." This is the smile of indispensable maternal recognition portrayed by centuries of artists in the grace-bearing Christian madonna or the Buddhist Kuan Yin.[6]

Co-Dependency and the Cults

An excess of acquiescence and infatuation cannot be missed in fictional women like Durga and Elizabeth, mentioned above. But this distortion is common among males, too, even when its presence is concealed by a blustering machismo. For any man who has to be admired by women, and play the swaggering custodian of women, depends on others for his very self-definition as a male. At any rate, in the Affective Way dependent personalities usually attach themselves to a partner with obvious, even exaggerated characteristics of the Activist Way. And eager to unfold and merge, they try to avoid anything disruptive of this close relationship. Though Freud's choice of the term "erotic" to describe such temperaments is misleading, he grasps their keynote: "Loving, but above all, being loved, is for them the most important thing in life. They are governed by dread about a loss of love, and this makes them peculiarly dependent on others who may withhold love from them."[7]

Today the media have prepared the public better than ever before to recognize victims from a co-dependent family, especially one scarred by sexual or substance abuse. Such people tend to grow up feeling unloved. This attitude is often compensated by an anxiety to prove lovable, ready to shoulder all the blame, even to the point of dismissing their own feelings. A friend of mine once asked me why he always gets depressed at the instant of success. It occurred to him that his own father, a recent suicide, had blundered so often in life, that only when the son failed, too, could these two strangers identify and communicate. The mother of one young woman was sometimes playful and hugging, but hateful when inebriated, screaming at her brood of unwanted pregnancies. "I'm recovering from years of physical tension," her daughter says today, "from the tensed shoulders holding fear, the constricted throat stopping my words . . . I used to shrivel up, to make myself small so that Mom would not notice me, so I would not offend her. My body carries the guilty conviction that I harmed her, ruined her life."[8]

Experiencing empathy for victims like these, you may underestimate the fierce survival instinct that often accompanies a painful dependency. Apparent subordination to another person sometimes disguises the need to dominate. A person's very weakness, so subservient and ingratiating, is often used to attract and hold on to a suitable protector. Hardened welfare recipients and all victims from an ingrained culture of poverty have had to master this lesson for survival.

This condition has been earmarked by Nietzsche as a pathological *ressentiment*, the whimpering slave morality of Jews and Christians. More accurately, it represents the attitude of any harassed minority, and may become the very martyr's badge of rebellion. For instance, a poet like Emily Dickinson manages to turn women's recessive position in the New England society of her day into a paradoxical artistic advantage. She plays at the role of child, a lark or bee, any neglected small creature, lost in her father's house or garden. But compressing herself into a miniature charge of energy, she explodes outward beyond all confinement.

Granted the intricate variations on this dependency pattern, an overly dependent personality seems the obvious target for one of the more aggressive religious cults. Without innuendo I shall apply the term *cult* to any voluntary group with relatively firm boundaries that exclude the outer world and bond those inside to intense religious commitment, usually under a leader with charism and authority. Today in the United States an unlikely alliance can be observed between many civil libertarians, psychiatrists, and mainline Churches, all reproachful of the body-snatching, brain-washing, and other criminally disruptive tactics attributed to many of the emergent cults. Often based on long-standing traditions elsewhere, most of these movements in America are newly arrived, or at least newly perceived.

In my own experience, I have been exposed to a spate of anti-cult films and concentration camp narratives by outraged ex-cultists. One of my clients, for instance, after abandoning his former cult membership with heavy anxiety and regret, has been harassed for years by phone calls and visits from scolding devotees. A handful of my former students seem to have shrunk into religious clones today, without the humor and humane self-critical attitudes I once enjoyed in them. Their conversation is now a sing-song cadence pattern of catchwords about some new twice-born vision, whether in Scientology, the Unification Church, or in Christian fundamentalist communities.

I think it cynical to argue that some young adults need imprisonment in order to prize what it means to be free. Nor do they need bombardment by others' dogmas before they can learn to appreciate their own ideas. I am convinced the duties and rights of each individual conscience are paramount, but with this lone proviso: no one may violate either the civil or wider human rights of another person. If a cult respects these rights, then it has earned the legal right to enlist any convert capable of a free decision. "There is wide variety in American religious taste," Justice Hugo Black remarked in his famous Ballard Case dissent of 1944. "The price for freedom of religion or of speech or of the press is that we must put up with, and even pay for, a good deal of rubbish."[9]

Though the cult experience may prove damaging because of unjust recruitment or retention tactics, perhaps blame must be distributed more fairly. I want to reaffirm a crucial psychological truism. The mature disciple must learn to resist projections from those with the distorted need to dominate. The mature guru, on the other hand, must learn to resist even more subtle projections from those with the distorted need to submit.

On any explicit religious quest, those with excessive dependency needs are prone to escape from one co-dependent family into another. Latching onto God, a cult, or a guru, they will tend to bask in a counterfeit solace there, or uncover new ways to manipulate their protectors. At its best, the cult may offer them the intimacy of a small commune for closer relationships they missed before. Or maybe by living with poor contemplatives, their cult membership may turn into an act of prophetic dissent against the consumer society that has long brain-washed their families.

Religious Self-Effacement

The aim of an excessive lover is to lose oneself in the loved one. Yet no one could be capable of such self-sacrifice but an idealized self, saintly and lovable, and so modest that these very endowments must be concealed. Karen Horney describes this personality type as shriveling in stature to avoid expansive moves, and feeling helpless, guilty, and unwanted. So eager to prove lovable, someone like this tends to be vulnerable to any show of warmth or interest, and to view all people as indiscriminately good. "Hence vindictive drives remain unconscious," she says, "and can only be expressed indirectly and in a disguised form."[10]

The god-image that inspires such self-immolation in believers is given their own prominent attributes of compassion and expendability. St. Paul describes God's incarnation in Jesus as a *kenosis* or self-emptying, laying aside his divine prerogatives: "he made himself nothing, he became a servant." Some Hindu genesis myths give a stunning account of the Creator's continuous self-abandonment. According to the Satapatha Brahmana text, he stands alone at the origin of all things, and experiencing no joy in self-contemplation, feels a yearning for companionship. "Let me sacrifice myself in living things, and all living things in myself,'' he says. And the world begins to take shape. But after creation, this sacred Oneness breaks apart. ''When he had fallen into pieces, his breath departed from the midst of him, and the gods abandoned him. He said to Agni, 'Put me, I pray you, together again.' '' Thus, the Creator has surrendered his primordial unity so that our multiple selves could come into existence. But now our burnt-offerings through Agni, god of fire, and a faithful moral life can help piece together the sacred cosmos.

In efforts to mirror this self-immolation of God, some believers try to wipe out their identity, even their earthly existence. Among some Hindus, for example, what begins with meticulous Vedic rituals may escalate to heroic mental discipline, bodily penance, self-mutilation, perhaps even suicide. In India and Nepal I have seen innumerable ragged figures, their bodies scarred and punctured, with legs often knotted in some frozen posture, usually begging and praying at temple thresholds. The classical Shaivite poet mystics of Southern India pray, ''I am Brahman. I offer myself in libation.'' Anecdotes from these lives show outrageous expendability. Disturbed at the bleeding eye of a Shiva statue, one man plucks out his own eye to offer in replacement. After the accidental loss of a food offering on the way to the temple, another slits his throat and surrenders his own life as food for Shiva.[11]

Portraying this same ideal in a less baroque context are the noble self-sacrificing animals of the Jataka tales, popular throughout Buddhist Southeast Asia. Each animal is a bodhisattva savior figure, representing the Buddha at an animal stage of evolution, before his later human incarnation as Gautama. A deer king, for instance, persuades a pregnant doe to let him replace her at the slaughtering block. A rabbit shakes the fleas from his pelt to spare their lives, and sacrifices his own life to the flames so that a fasting brahmin can enjoy his meal without having to slay animals.

Saints and Anorexics

Self-annihilation has also left its imprint on the Christian tradition. According to one inventory today, half the forty canonized women saints in thirteenth-century Italy almost died from excessive fasting. For instance, if any particle of food remained in the stomach of Catherine of Siena during her fast before receiving the Eucharist, she would induce vomiting. Clare of Assisi, her feet unshod, her bed always on the ground, succeeded in starving herself to the point of serious illness. All these women manifested a robust eagerness to care for others, without letting others take care of them. As news of their dramatic austerities swept Europe, they became exemplars for many noble women, who soon abandoned their wealth, initiated severe bouts of fasting, wore hairshirts, and either became nuns or formed pacts of mutual continence with their husbands.[12]

A familiar narrative recurs in most of these twenty biographies: the young virgin's precocious spirituality, admired by her affluent parents, eventually alarms them as she gets older, pressing her fasts and self-denial to extremes. Neither the family nor an admonitory chorus of clerics and confessors, all trying to break her will, can encourage the woman to moderate this resolute fasting. By the fourteenth century, however, Church authorities felt reluctant to canonize women for no other moral or religious accomplishments than this athletic piety of self-starvation. Fasting for its own sake might just be slow suicide, stubborn pride, perhaps a mask of Satan.

Interesting parallels arise between these medieval fasting saints, Victorian hysterics, and contemporary anorexics. Applying the limited insight of today about hysteria and anorexia as a sort of grid transparency, and hoping to avoid reductivism, the cultural historian can underline features in thirteenth century asceticism that might otherwise look random and incoherent.

All three disorders center on drastic bodily symptoms and seem to claim women more than men. Impatient therapists and spiritual directors sense beneath any recovery agreement a secret contest of wills against anyone trying to intervene. The high and low public tide of all three can be charted like an epidemic. Mild forms of each disorder shade off into what their respective societies consider the normal feminine ideal. Extreme forms lampoon this ideal, at times endangering the woman's life.

To begin with, the nineteenth-century hysteric and the current anorexic look like opposites, the first charming and pliable, the second tough and severely disciplined.[13] Yet on deeper analysis, both are often incomplete women, willfully one-sided, without the corresponding endowments. Perhaps in all three disorders, women are driven by their respective society's expectations now toward, now against, the Way of Action. They become trapped in destructive measures of compliance and self-effacement.

The ideal of femininity which a classical hysteric embodied and also parodied subversively can be gathered from a catalog of stock "complaints" treated by family medicine in the nineteenth century. Green Sickness, for example, meant chronic constipation in women, an ailment some doctors attributed to worries about flatulence, and thus to an excessive contraction of the buttocks. And White Sickness meant paleness of skin from seclusion indoors, mostly to avoid the prying gaze of strangers. Most of the women hysterics analyzed by Breuer and Freud suffered repressions against careless expression of bodily needs or feelings. Their social role required virginity, purity, and uncompromising marital fidelity. Yet their symptoms of paralysis, amnesia, seizure, and other histrionics functioned as an oblique defiance and cry for attention.

Today this dramatic vocabulary of hysteria appears to have receded in most Eurocentric societies. However, it still flourishes among some of our minorities, and even more so in those Third World cultures that prize an indirect, nonverbal expression of emotions. The less advantaged everywhere, too, learn that drastic physical symptoms, not subtle verbal complaints, get them hospital attention and unemployment compensation. On the surface, however, present standards of femininity in the United States seem to offer most women a more immediate, verbal expression for their needs.

Yet the modern prevalence of women anorexics suggests otherwise. Though this affliction occurs worldwide in a wide diversity of character types, it confines itself mostly to affluent societies that have not yet resolved an important role discrepancy. Young girls in our own culture, for example, are expected to show the carefree vivacity of Scarlett O'Hara and all those other endearing traits of centuries ago that we still value in our children. By age nine, envying the figure of toy Olympic gymnast, most girls have already begun their first diet. But an adult woman professional today must look and work like Hillary Rodham Clinton in a chic executive role. Unlike the self-indulgent hysteric, who could codify all her mental repressions by exuberant body language, today's anorexic has to cope with a womanly ideal of self-denial and achievement. This is a new secular asceticism.

Today as a young girl moves into adolescence and early adulthood, she must train herself to be expendable for others, disciplined and autonomous, with a lean, attractive body. She is often tempted to shrink back from adult sexuality and responsibility, or take on too much at once. Biochemical and family pathogenic factors, of course, might predispose a young woman for this disorder. But society itself offers its own teasing ambushes: dietary fads, petite-sized fashions, aerobics and physical fitness regimens, the allure of high achievement and autonomy, at least over one's own body. The anorexic is an embarrassing caricature of the superwoman our culture now esteems so highly. A workaholic heroine, self-sufficient and self-denying, yet unable to admit her own needs and desires, she may be reduced at last to the martyrdom of forced feeding.

Juxtaposed with hysterics and anorexics, the twenty medieval women saints seem to represent a third flawed attempt to salvage some autonomy in a world that permitted them almost none at all. The preaching of Sts. Dominic and Francis, the rise of guilds, urban workers, and the middle class, all these led to revitalized models of sanctity. Earlier centuries had focused on abbots, kings, and those of ostensible power, yet the thirteenth century now idealized more laymen and laywomen as potential saints. Encouraged by this spiritual renewal to aspire heavenward with new passion, a devout woman might emulate even the ancient desert ascetics in a spiritual marathon. Since her patriarchal culture excluded a woman from most power roles, and also from the Activist Way to sanctity, she was left at least her own body, over which she could exercise power. Perhaps much of her spiritual generosity toward others betrayed this same one-sided, controlling edge, ministering to others' needs, not as they actually were, but only as she defined them.

Medieval Church leaders and other men of the era, rhapsodizing over the sublime image of Mary, yearned to shield the average woman, less privileged than the Virgin, from her own vulnerable sensuality. Perhaps in derisive commentary on this sort of male presumption, and as a parody of genuine saintly heroines like Sts. Clare and Catherine, some women could respond by eradicating in their own bodies any promise of beauty or desire whatsoever. Their body symbolism acted out a homily to the medieval world: is this sexless skeleton the only woman to satisfy you? Medieval churchmen, like frustrated modern therapists, all representing the male establishment, found themselves summoned again and again to sickbeds. They would soon exhaust every bribery and threat to break a resolute course of self-destruction.

Self-Denial, Self-Immolation

The modern counterparts to medieval religious extremity are Gandhi's later hunger fasts for Hindu-Muslim reconciliation. Nehru himself viewed such tactics as extortion—the exercise of tyrannical will, with little respect for mature democratic choice among Gandhi's own followers. We might also include those prison hunger strikes today that are staged in explicit religio-political protest, but especially the controversial starvation of philosopher Simone Weil.

Pleading without success to be accepted as a fighter in the French Resistance, Weil died of tuberculosis and self-starvation at a British hospital in 1943 at age thirty-four. One reason she gave for refusal of food and tube feeding was a gesture of solidarity with those on limited rations under Nazi occupation. Her books and journals are those of a unique tormented conscience, an intellectual Jewish-Christian mystic turned social activist, trying to live a spirituality of harsh poverty and abandonment. Recognizing in her own faith the impassioned dualism of Albigensian and Manichean heretics, she identifies her spirituality by the paradoxical term *de-creation.*[14]

An analysis of food and hunger symbolism in her writings discloses a bizarre preoccupation, even at moments of profound religious vision. The soul is hungry, and faith is nourishment. On earth you love God best in emptiness, dispossession, hunger—an endless waiting for grace, as in the fiction of Kafka and Beckett. "The Virgin's milk, the Father's seed—I shall have it if I cry for it." She prays to be divested of all worldly desires, "devoured by God, transformed into Christ's substance, and given for food to afflicted men whose body and soul lack every kind of nourishment. And let me be a paralytic—blind, deaf, witless, and utterly decrepit." Though these images belong to the stock vocabulary of Christian mystics, in Weil they soon become incessant and self-punishing.

The following passage reads almost like a text for Aztec rites of human sacrifice. Looking for God, the weary soul "with nothing to eat or drink, separated from his dear ones . . . will arrive at the center of the labyrinth. And there God is waiting to eat him. Later the soul will go out again, but he will be changed, he will have become different, after being eaten and digested by God."

I think Weil's eating disorder became an overworked metaphor for insatiable spiritual longing. Once she could starve and empty herself totally, perhaps her deranged mind did imagine the soul would merge or be incorporated literally into God. Or denied an activist role as saboteur against the Nazis, she may have turned her own spiritual and physical self-effacement into an agency of destructive protest, much like Gandhi's hunger strikes. Or was she still wrestling with parental authority—once an excessively compliant daughter, now destroying all reminders of her parents' food and clothing? At times her mind seems entranced with affliction for its own sake. Despite all her insistence on waiting patiently, Weil's body rushes headlong toward a God expected to respond on her own violent terms.

The biography of Weil by psychologist Robert Coles recounts an interview with Anna Freud, after she had examined all the Weil sources gathered for his book. With exemplary hesitation to diagnose, she admits feeling overwhelmed by the breadth of this woman's personal and intellectual involvements, especially throughout such a brief life. The range of a clinical anorexic's interests, on the contrary, would have shrunk to more self-centered limits. For Weil was not pathologically fixated on her own appearance, weight, appetite, or potential obesity.

''My hunch is that if she had a mirror,'' Anna Freud concludes, ''she would have given that mirror the same trouble she gave a loaf of bread! At the same time, her heart was ready to travel all over the world, reach out to everyone, it seems, and carry with it, if she could, her frail, exhausted body.''[15]

In a letter one year before her death, Weil acknowledged that she viewed her own existence ''directly and continuously as an evil . . . I absolutely cannot imagine the possibility that any human being could feel friendship for me.'' She then begins to doubt the soundness of her own religious impulses. Whereas Christ asks his followers to deny themselves, and expects self-annihilation to be hard, Weil has always found it too easy. She recalls suffering at one time in her life so much mental and physical affliction, that suicide seemed ''my imperative duty.'' Yet at that moment, while completely unprepared for it, she felt ''a presence more personal, more certain, and more real than that of a human being. It was inaccessible both to sense and to imagination, and it resembled the love that irradiates the tenderest smile of somebody one loves.''[16]

Here in this woman's candid self-description are an incredible juxtaposition of many authentic and counterfeit motifs treated in the present chapter on affectivity. Dying in loving solidarity with other human beings. Activism paralyzed by self-loathing and an overly dependent waiting on God. A tendency to misuse religious conventions for rationalizing a distorted sense of self-denial. And yet despite these queasy foundations, there is an instant of self-transcendence—perhaps genuine, perhaps delusional. The unexpected visit from a loving God.

7
Way of Contemplation

In the United States the Activist Way has shaped our cultural perspective to such an extent that people often remain unaware or intolerant of other spiritualities, especially the Way of Contemplation.

There is a Carmelite monastery of strictly enclosed contemplative nuns, for instance, located a few steps from the University of San Francisco. Just singing and praying all day, these women never leave the grounds, and no doubt take great risks in trying to live out this Way with such intensity. Since the sisters do not teach or engage in any other social work, why should anyone subsidize them, and how can their lives be of any mortal use? I am often questioned about the rationale for their existence, but have no handy reply. Since I lack their particular contemplative calling, I could scarcely live that demanding routine without serious mental impairment. Moreover, it is ironical that the questioner probably does not appreciate even my own activist religious commitment on its own terms. For both the nuns and I are accustomed to be measured by our secular usefulness to society, sometimes as just one more potential salary or tax return.

Apologia for Contemplatives

A shrewd six-panel cartoon by Jules Feiffer spells out the common activist bias against a contemplative life. Crew-cut, wearing a black turtleneck and suitcoat, the stereotyped activist of western spirituality has a rugged, beefy profile. But the contemplative of eastern spirituality seems to have curvature of the spine, a lean shoulderless torso, with glasses, long silken hair, and a simpering smile. In an exchange between these two, each phase begins with the meek figure's affirmation about his god-image, followed by a quick counter-claim by his aggressive partner. "My God is an eastern God—hip, cool, contemplative." And the other responds, "My God is a western God—aggressive, macho, a go-getter."

Subsequent panels of the cartoon affirm that the eastern God keeps you resigned to inevitable failure, and offsets material anxieties with cosmic numbness. On the contrary, though the western God clobbers you with guilt if you don't make it, he is easy on redemption if you cut a few corners. Yet in a final reversal, the activist's bored anticipations are shattered by a sudden disclosure: "My eastern God grossed 40 million tax-free last year." With eyes popping, the activist counters, "Are you sure your eastern God isn't my western God in drag?"

Feiffer's sketch demonstrates again the extent to which culture and temperament influence differing images of the sacred. It also unmasks the casual imperialism exercised by an activist point of view. Notice that the westerner in this script is dealt all the pert rejoinders. Even his grudging respect at last for the contemplative viewpoint rests solely on his own tough empirical criteria. For the easterner's religious alternative can initiate not only a successful business, but also a tax shelter.

To win recognition, even the right to survive, contemplatives have to withstand countless pressures toward activist conformity. However, their most relentless opponent is not the hard-nosed materialist caricatured above, but the religious leader with an alien mindset, often from the contemplative's own Church tradition. Kenneth Kaunda, former President of Zambia, recognizes this clash between two distinctive mentalities in his own religious background, the organizational and the visionary. Educated in Christian colonial schools, he has observed in his own adult personality a dialectic between what he labels the European and the African dimensions. He tends to separate his Eurocentric problem-solving mind from his Primal situation-experiencing heart—alternatives reminiscent of Gabriel Marcel's distinction between a puzzle to be solved and a mystery to be contemplated.

Kaunda's European mindset, logical and Faustian, is needed to balance the budget or split the atom. But his African mindset is poetic and holistic, indispensable to keep his relationships truly human. The first attitude is either-or, unable to live with opposing ideas until they get somehow reconciled. But the second attitude is both-and. This posture accepts a fruitful tension between opposites—between God and the natural world, for example, or even between old Primal traditions and the new imported Christian faith. For Kaunda, both the European and African dimensions in himself need each other to constitute a complete human being. He wisely resists the impulse to embrace a one-sided African contemplation as the noble antithesis to a one-sided Eurocentric activism.[1]

The previous three chapters have contended that no sacred Way can be lived maturely without all three components—a balancing activism, affectivity, and contemplation. This is notably true of the Contemplative Way. For as its essence rarefies, so it falls more readily into self-caricature—the lone Stylites squatting in manure, the swami on a bed of spikes, or the bearded guru chauffeured in a fleet of Rolls Royces. Genuine contemplation can be appreciated best, not in dramatic isolation, but as the indispensable component in a rounded human life.

The recovery of this neglected dimension is exemplified in "Goose Pond," a widely anthologized short story by Thomas Williams.[2] Robert Hurley, long grieving over the death of his wife from cancer, leaves family and grandchildren for a retreat and solitary deer hunt in the New Hampshire mountains. After days of meditating, and at last by the act of slaying and skinning a doe, he manages in a ritual way to do something in retrospect about his wife's final six months of terrible pain. Like geese settling for the night at Goose Pond, Hurley has realized his need to touch down for respite before resuming the bracing, dangerous journey ahead. This silent experience in the mountains replenishes his life with the lost undercurrent of meaning and order, without which he had become an automaton.

As another illustration of a restored life, I have in mind an elderly Jesuit friend, once a manifest workaholic and hidden alcoholic, performing superbly at any donkey-work assigned him. He had turned into a thin-skinned old man, a domineering clown and raconteur. Yet since his recovery in Alcoholics Anonymous, he has recently proved more relaxed, approachable, ready to listen. You recognize that the careers of great concert pianists like Horowitz or Rubenstein do not spiral up steadily, but often break off suddenly in mid-career. Even people so gifted need a fallow period, sometimes lasting many years, to refine their experience or technique. In a comparable way, my priest friend spends a few quiet hours daily feeding the squirrels and ducks in a nearby park, or meditating. He has come to relish each chance for companionship and work, but also for solitude. In his life this missing ingredient, now reclaimed, is what I mean by the contemplative dimension.

Like chapters 5 and 6, the present chapter maps out this particular spirituality at its maturity and also at its nadir. Attention centers first on the contemplative ideal and god-image, then potential imbalances of religious withdrawal, solipsism, and depression.

A God of Wonder and Silence

In all religious traditions the contemplative emphasis implies a visionary delight in the sacred for its own sake. To single out this profound gaze, Buddhist artists often give buddhas and bodhisattvas a third eye in the middle of their forehead—the wise penetrating gaze of the Hindu god Shiva. Yet Sikh calendar art, for example, takes a reverse approach. Its ten canonized gurus are often portrayed with eyes almost white, the pupil disappearing beneath the upper lid, implying blindness. Thus, each artistic convention suggests that ordinary vision is expanded or eclipsed by inner enlightenment.

The contemplative turns to God as more than a divine co-worker or lover—images suitable to the Ways of Action and Affectivity. Now the sacred confronts you as a mystery to be experienced in its full reality, just for its own sake.

When Rudolph Otto describes the sacred as *mysterium tremendum et fascinosum,* he means an unfathomable source that evokes shuddering awe at the same instant as loving ecstasy. Attempts to probe into such a paradox have always challenged the imagination. In the Bible, for example, God's loving fidelity guarantees his covenants, but his wrath, irrational and terrifying, sometimes erupts to make him regret and smash all guarantees. With similar ambivalence, the Hindu God Vishnu, extending two of his four arms, beckons with a conch shell in one hand to welcome devotees, a flaming discus in the other to demolish those who reject his summons. And Julian of Norwich, telling of her first mystical experience, gropes for a language to pin down this "strange harmony of contrasts." It was "living and vivid and hideous and fearful and sweet and lovely."

Not just the sacred but the entire universe is a visionary marvel to the contemplative. Jhabvala's short story on the three Ways, introduced in chapter 4, identifies in each Way a differing approach to natural beauty. The activist Margaret delights to recall her trips by bus, train, cycle, rickshaw, or even bullock cart, anything to reach the most inaccessible temple or cave or tomb. She must get to see everything of worth in India, and wants to tell everyone about it. "What will you ever know," she admonishes Elizabeth, "if you stay in one place all the time!" Elizabeth longs to see most of these natural wonders, and can imagine them vividly, but the only trips yet outside Delhi have been visits with her husband's family in Ankhpur. Margaret may know one India, but Elizabeth surely knows another. She has learned much from living with an indigenous Indian family, but especially with Raju himself. Her passionate, and perhaps idolatrous, commitment to the Way of Affectivity can be summed up in one line: "Yes, Raju was her India!"

Unlike both women, however, the contemplative Babaji, from what little the reader learns about him, seems overwhelmed by the beauty of Nature for its own sake. When he invites Elizabeth to his hermitage in Almora, he tries eagerly to describe the mountains, trees, clouds, the grandeur and peace. But "words failed him and he could only spread his hands farther and smile into the distance, as if he saw a beautiful vision there."

Words are sometimes an enemy to both Activist and Contemplative Ways, but on different grounds. Instead of lending an active hand to help someone up after a fall, you may substitute an abortive gesture or polite excuse. Throughout life you may prove yourself someone who can only sympathize, coach, or moralize. Words at best have the power to animate bodily movement, but they can also paralyze it, pretending that you must have acted, just because you spoke.

Yet words trouble a sensitive poet like Rilke, on the contrary, for more complex aesthetic and spiritual reasons. Like Adam in the Book of Genesis, all poets are namers by vocation, and every new act of poetic creation should be an exacting rite of homage and contemplation. As a child, Rilke used to name God with casual familiarity in his prayers. But in adult life, "you would scarcely ever hear me name him. There is an indescribable discretion between us, and where once there was nearness and penetration, there stretch new distances." Instead of union and possession, Rilke feels a genuine bond, but also a sacred "namelessness."[3]

The focus of this poet's awe can be associated here with the perennial apophatic viewpoint explained in chapter 3. Many mystics prefer to evoke a sense of the sacred by separating it from everything it cannot be: the In-finite, Im-mutable, In-effable. For instance, Gautama the Buddha describes nirvana as "the Isle of No-beyond, where there is No-thing to be grasped." In some prayer traditions, too, words function not as discourse, but as the evocative background music of mantra and glossolalia. Rilke prefers an attitude of disciplined speechlessness mostly because he cannot bear to see catchwords of religiosity replace an actual experience of the sacred. In a similar way, most contemplatives, like Babaji in Jhabvala's story, hesitate to let stock epithets, a snapshot, or the mere checkmark on a traveler's itinerary substitute for an appreciation of the place or event, each with its unique identity.

Since the sacred transcends all human efforts to name it, perhaps the appropriate setting for contemplation is silence. A young mother, for example, writes about upheavals in her spiritual life after the birth of two children. She must yield now to each child's time needs and cannot organize her own day as freely as before. But she is learning new ways to pray—speechless moments, just being present to God, with nothing particular to be accomplished. She is helped by remembering "the wordless presence of my children in the same room with me. It is so stirring and so immediate, that to distract that event with words would be to dilute the loveliness of the experience." She calls this moment "an understanding that lets two hearts beat almost as one." She has recovered a fresh sense of wonder, too. Now she is discovering the world through a child's eyes, giving each detail undivided attention. Every crack in the sidewalk is examined for blades of grass and ants, and then fondled by hands eager to touch all these new guests. "The trip from the front door of the house to the car was an adventure in unmasking the glory of God in its minute splendor."[4]

Thus, the contemplative temperament aims, not at the top of the biggest firm or university, but at the center in oneself—a balanced human ideal of working and leisure combined. In the teaching of Zen masters, contemplative mindfulness or enlightenment means that when you walk, you fully walk, and when you eat, you fully eat. Your mind is not focused on rewards lying ahead or above—the Marxist future classless utopia, for instance, or a supra-natural heaven. Gandhi insists on *nishkama karma*, action without selfish desire, without reward. Whether you pray or work, the deed is already full of meaning, and must not be viewed as just a means to something else. Eternity and salvation begin in the immediate present. According to the Gospel of John, God's Kingdom is already here and now. "Philip," Jesus says, "whoever sees me has seen the Father." Each Sabbath for the Jew is even now a share in God's *shekhinah* or glory. And for Mahayana Buddhists the daily experience of alienation is already nirvana, not yet aware of itself.

As insisted before, any comprehensive spirituality must find room for a contemplative component. Yet only certain people have the temperament and developmental history requisite for adopting the Way of Contemplation itself, rather than a spirituality of action or affectivity. Most of all, the mature contemplative must have an extraordinary sense of play, imagination, and mystery, and a talent for creative regression. Developmental psychologist D. H. Winnicott traces these endowments back to the child's earliest successful encounters with what he calls "transitional space."

To ease separation from the mother, a child creates various transitional objects—thumb, security blanket, doll, teddy bear, or some imaginary companion. This symbolic space is neither a realm of pure illusion nor of hard empirical fact. It involves both inner creation and outer discovery. As Winnicott explains it: "In health the infant creates what is in fact lying around, waiting to be found. . . . Yet the object must be found in order to be created." This intermediate realm in childhood is a matrix for later intense experiences belonging "to the arts, to religion, to imaginative living, and to creative scientific work."

Parents, family, and the surrounding culture must learn to treat the transitional object and space with ritualistic respect. Once the child's private talisman or first intimations of the sacred are acknowledged, they can become the basis for a maturing contemplative disposition. Erikson calls attention to the way parents greet, name, pick up, and cuddle a child—repeated patterns that shape the course of life-long ritual expectations. "This first and dimmest affirmation," he concludes, "this sense of a hallowed presence, contributes to human ritual-making a pervasive element which we will call the numinous . . . a sense of separateness transcended, and yet also of distinctiveness confirmed."[5]

Contemplative Distortions

The mature contemplative life requires equanimity and balance—time for engagement in work or friendship, and time, too, for disengagement. Most important, to befriend oneself more intensively, or to meditate, there must be some measure of withdrawal from the everyday world. But gestures of disengagement, of course, will often be judged antisocial or threatening. One early evening I took a meditative walk alone through the safe residential neighborhood of a large city. It had struck me that modern urban existence offers little space for quiet and solitude—rooftops, dark empty churches, parks just in daytime. A patrol car suddenly pulled up to the pavement where I was walking. The police suspected a possible criminal, victim, or suicide. It looked abnormal to be wandering out alone.

The three contemplative disorders to be examined all involve excessive self-concern and isolation from others. These counterfeits might be called narcissistic, except that the term in current usage has been inflated to identify almost any harmful, and even constructive, focus on the self.

Religious Avoidance

Chapter 6 explored a tendency in overly dependent lovers toward self-effacement and even self-disfigurement. And chapter 4, too, mentioned the temptation after mental breakdown to consolidate losses by constricting one's space to that of a more bland personality. Less seriously disturbed than these examples, however, a wider range of people have been damaged no less by earlier failure, loss, or infringement on their personality. They have learned since then to pare down their dreams and needs. As the gallows-humor motto on my colleague's office door puts it, "I feel a lot better, now that I've abandoned all hope." Some have deliberately or unconsciously built a citadel to withstand that most threatening of all counterfeits in the Active and Affective Ways—domination or engulfment by another person. Their aim is to keep committed personal relationships at a distance, and avoid interference from any social institution.

Such an act of renunciation can give a false impression of integrity and self-sufficiency. Psychologist Heinz Kohut commends a "new, expanded, transformed, and cosmic" narcissism embodied by the heroic Roman Stoics, in contrast to more sterile forms of self-centredness. These ancient Romans do not display resignation and hopelessness, but "quiet pride, often coupled with mild disdain of the rabble. . . . A non-isolated, creative superiority which judges and admonishes with quiet assurance." Yet the nuances here of superior disdain cannot be explained away. These are the same distortions that trouble me in the Nicomachean Ethics, where Aristotle personifies his highest ideals in the so-called Magnanimous Man, a figure so large-hearted that he would never stoop to anything petty or unworthy. His lofty self-image must never risk being tarnished.[6]

Self-diffidence, renunciation of family and possessions, and detachment from cravings of the flesh are all gestures suitable for nominal spiritual endorsement. In fact, the life of monastic withdrawal is encouraged by many religious traditions, with their own differing equivalents for what Christians call permanent vows of obedience, poverty, and chastity. These promises can be viewed as an act of both negation and affirmation. You abandon personal independence, material possessions, sexual expression and spouse, in order to turn more intensively to the sacred. Or in another sense, through your own dedication you render sacred the fundamental human quest for freedom, wealth, and love.

A vowed contemplative commitment, however, may prove dangerously enticing for the avoidant personality. This is the sort of person who at last surrenders to God the gifts rejected by everyone else. As theologian John Courtney Murray observes, you risk purposelessness, irresponsibility, and selfish regression, if you do not keep these vows in their integrity. Under the mask of obedience you could become dependent and inert, without aspiration or assertion or creativity, sparing yourself the agonies of decision. In a situation of poverty or communal sharing of property, you could live a secure parasitic life, insulated from the dignity of responsible work. And behind the facade of chastity, you could become lonely, crotchety, emotionally childish and self-enclosed, a disembodied head. "To be a human being in any walk of life is not easy. Few achieve full virility, full womanhood either. . . . The world puts obstacles in the way. . . . Religion does, too. And there are those who succumb to the obstacles."[7]

This book so far has identified various immature motives for membership in a cult or fundamentalist sect—notably, the urge to serve and be cherished by a strong spiritual leader, or to seek a paranoid bulwark against the religious enemy. Now the rationale of escape offers a third excuse—hiding in the shadow of a group, the hankering for an oasis of religious integrity. To find contemplative solitude, you may long for an exclusive religious circle, so elite that it eventually excludes everyone but yourself.

For example, the last years of Evelyn Waugh's life were aggravated by self-imposed isolation, resistant to innovations in Catholic ritual introduced after the late fifties. His novelette *The Ordeal of Gilbert Pinfold,* in the portrait of its central character, approximates this same viewpoint. Pinfold abhors everything that happened in his own lifetime. The tiny kindling of charity that comes to him through his religious tradition is sufficient just to temper his disgust. Pinfold's habit is to seek the least frequented Mass and avoid all church organizations. "At the very time when the leaders of his Church were exhorting their people to emerge from the catacombs into the forum, to make their influence felt in democratic politics and to regard worship as a corporate rather than a private act, Pinfold burrowed ever deeper into the rock."[8]

A familiar parable in the Gospel of Matthew advises the Christian community to wait till final harvest for separating weeds from wheat, or else risk destroying the wheat. Yet there have always been zealots who yearn for a premature winnowing of God's elect. A decade ago, the spiritual leader of a local Pentecostal community felt chosen to organize a disruptive exodus, relocating families two thousand miles away. Left behind were those in the original group judged to have insufficient religious stamina and promise. I happened to be one counselor at hand, expected to help console some of the survivors, most of them crushed and bitter. Though any sectarian's passion for integrity is understandable, its obvious backside is a predisposition against the drop-out, the partly-in, and the outsider. Yet I am convinced a balanced spirituality must reach beyond incest and spiritual cloning, to a genuine love for the stranger, the other person as *other.*

Behind the fastidious spirituality of a Tory squire, or the superior remoteness of a Roman Stoic, there often stands a shy introvert, fending off an extrovert world from some guarded corner of privacy. The common excesses in this temperament are a sense of inferiority, over-sensitivity, and awkwardness in forming relationships. Introvert disorders of this sort, called *shinkeishitsu* by the Japanese, have long received special attention in Morita therapy. Under Dr. Morita's regime, patients usually begin with a week of lonely bed rest in a clinic or hospital, without any distractions but their own thoughts. The surfeit of self-focus, which at first enchants them, in a few days becomes an unendurable bore. For the next few weeks, they eagerly displace this concern from themselves onto details of some assigned task, such as chopping wood, gardening, or carpentry, and gradually, a few limited games and conversations.

The premise behind this Morita technique of re-socialization is a specific Buddhist teaching. You stop the flow of consciousness, flood it, or redirect it in order to precipitate a breakthrough beyond the conventional ego. This is the path toward a deeper Buddha-realization. You learn to be fully present in each task and personal interaction at hand. In other words, a withdrawn pseudo-contemplative learns step by step the authentic contemplative path of the Zen tea ceremony—a spirituality of the immediate and particular.[9]

Religious Gluttony

Religious gluttony, the second contemplative counterfeit to be examined, is described by St. John of the Cross as an exaggerated focus on the moment of ecstatic illumination. Beginners in the spiritual life are especially vulnerable to this blight. "These persons think their own satisfaction and pleasure are the satisfaction and service of God." It does not take much to render them faint-hearted and negligent in meditation. Soon they lose all motivation to pray. Their first priority is "to do what they themselves are inclined to do. So it would probably be more profitable for them not to engage in these exercises at all."[10]

In many households since the innovating sixties, name-brands of the major historical religious traditions have been replaced by a home-recipe spirituality. Worship a la carte may now include a statue of Jesus or Krishna, candles and flowers, massage and yoga, a ritual meal or quiet period of meditation, and a few texts from mystics of East and West. On occasion some guests gather to celebrate Passover, Chinese New Year's, Buddha's Birthday, Christmas, the Winter Solstice, or the close of Ramadan—a single feast or all in sequence—but without commitment to any particular creed or community. Yet no more dramatic antithesis to the uncompromising spiritual austerity of John of the Cross could be imagined than this laid-back improvisational milieu. Here Christian asceticism, Hindu yoga, the Shinto martial arts, Zen Buddhist exercise and teaching, all these vital traditions can be trimmed down to a spiritual placebo for the immature.

The Zen mystique, for instance, has been adopted by many in Europe and America for snob-appeal, as the popular Zen theologian Alan Watts acknowledges. These disciples often invest the Soto, Rinzai, or other Zen schools of Japan with the same institutional authority already repudiated in their own Eurocentric religious heritage. Today a few weeks in a Kyoto monastery or Zen training seminar, or the diploma from a martial arts academy, certify the spiritual expatriate in some eyes as an established contemplative.

Even a flexible guru like Watts cannot stomach the cheap bohemian caricatures of genuine Zen practice. He conjures up the most despicable figure he can imagine—a ''cool, fake-intellectual hipster searching for kicks, name-dropping bits of Zen and jazz jargon to justify a disaffiliation from society which is in fact just ordinary, callous exploitation of other people.''[11]

A famous refrain from novelist Jack Kerouac's personal philosophy typifies the listless hipster attitude: ''I don't know. I don't care. And it doesn't make any difference.'' No doubt many have adopted the Zen facade merely to justify sheer caprice in art and in life, as if ''anything goes,'' and to rebel, trash, or escape. The context of hostile diffidence surrounding Kerouac's words, however, is far removed from the serenity of authentic Zen detachment. Master Hakuin, for instance, was once accused by a young girl of fathering her child. ''Is that so?'' the Master says calmly. Later, after everyone takes her side, she apologizes for lying. But told of her retraction, Hakuin, with the same equanimity as before, just turns back to his earlier response, ''Is that so?''

As most Zen masters insist, a thorough satori enlightenment is the rarest achievement, in Japan or anywhere else. For it calls for a radical spiritual conversion, a turning aside from selfishness. Some Rinzai Buddhists, for example, are denounced by other Zen schools for their alleged pursuit of the elusive satori ecstasy itself, missing its more permanent moral implications. The target for a similar critique is Chogyam Trungpa, the Naropa Institute, and his Buddhist ashram at Boulder, Colorado. Untouched by the classical Buddhist emphasis on responsible compassion toward sentient life, his Vajrayanist disciples appear to be ''set free of moral constraint, in which all action is seen as play . . . For the most part, moral and social questions disappear from all discourse, even from idle conversation . . . Nothing could be further from their sensibility than the notion of a free community of equals or a just society or the common good.''[12]

Even the psychologist Abraham Maslow, despite his earlier uncritical enthusiasm, acknowledges some second thoughts about this fascination with peak experiences as "the only or at least the highest good of life, giving up other criteria of right and wrong." Enchanted by an instant of joy and wonder, you may be tempted to turn away "from the world and from other people in the search for triggers to peak-experiences, any triggers." The higher states of consciousness then tend to become so paramount that they must be bargained for on schedule with drugs and magic. Too impatient for steady religious training or a discerning guru, you may never pause to distinguish conscience from harmful impetuosity. And the worst dangers ahead, Maslow warns, are sadism and loss of compassion.[13]

Among my friends and colleagues I have witnessed many roundabout spiritual and geographic quests by those trying to get permanently stoned on the sacred. Preoccupied with visions or dreams, some shut themselves up in the desert, others in their condominiums. Though it can seldom be confirmed, a few promising students in my classes each semester seem to be trading their minds for a psychedelic short-cut to ecstasy. Some years ago, one client recounted with bitterness how her father had abandoned a wife and three young children for an American Hindu desert hermitage, just to "find himself." In Nepal I met one group of middle-aged hippies on a world trek, belittling local people and their culture, and searching for the perfect, ecologically pure mountain vista. They treated Nepali villagers as one vast laboratory to indulge their tourist experiments in self-realization.

Characterizing himself with mocking self-disparagement as a spiritual gourmet, a wealthy student of mine once flew to India, eager to locate some ashram where he could attain a drug-free experience of ecstasy. But watching his India mystique dissolve in the heat and smells confronting him on arrival at the Calcutta air terminal, he fled home two hours later on the first accessible plane. A Catholic nun friend signs up for every retreat and workshop in sight, accumulates the familiar classics on prayer, and allots increasingly longer periods to daily meditation. Though keeping an intensive spiritual journal for years, she has complained recently that all this effort seems to have generated so little genuine self-understanding and kindness. Neglecting friends, work, even her personal appearance, she dreads that each day might soon be lived just to become a later journal entry. With no loss of self-critical humor, she has given this malaise a name—her outer circle of hell, the vanity of self-absorption.

Religious Depression

God's remedy for spiritual gluttony and other obstacles to maturity is the Dark Night experience. According to John of the Cross, it arrives inevitably, a gift of gentle spiritual weaning. Though adrift in an arid wilderness, and sensing God's eclipse or absence, you should realize God is just releasing you from his arms, prodding you to learn how to walk alone. "For God sets them in this Night only to prove them and to humble them, and to reform their desires, so that they go on, not nurturing in themselves a sinful gluttony in spiritual things."

John's interpretation of this depression reinforces the advice offered by mystics in other traditions. Zen masters, for instance, mention phases of *makyo,* literally the "region of evil"—unmanageable anxiety, fears, violent and suicidal impulses. You are coached to let all these demons from the unconscious surface patiently, and to live with them as a providential handicap in the arduous spiritual quest.[14]

In my own experience there is no ready yardstick to distinguish this Dark Night experience from neurochemical depressive disorders, or from more prosaic bouts with aridity, cynicism, and existential despair. When John of the Cross describes Dark Nights of both the senses and the spirit, he mentions distaste and fear, sadness, loss of meaning, dullness of the eye and ear, torpor and despair. But these symptoms are reported in almost any depressive situation. The mild occasional episode, of course, is clearly not a drastic prolonged one. I cannot forget the reaction of an elderly spiritual director, when I knocked at his door thirty years ago as a young high school teacher, suffering momentary burn-out. I complained that this desolation felt like my own Dark Night. "Let's work with a less melodramatic premise," he interrupted with a smile. "You're just spiritually lazy and tepid, or you're neurotic." Then he offered me, not some religious bromide, but an actual pill. It came from the daily medication prescribed by his doctor for this priest's own depression, a serious disorder.

Whereas some people may exaggerate their depressive symptoms, as I no doubt did on that occasion, it is disastrous to underestimate them. The victim often recognizes something is wrong, but seems unable or reluctant to put it into words. Disclosure feels like an admission of cowardice or sin. Perhaps you have been taught that if God is on your side, what have you to fear? Thus, the standard religious advice for depressives is often simply to believe and pray more firmly, shift focus away from oneself, and trust the remedy of positive thinking.

As a counselor, and also as the member of a large aging Jesuit community, I have learned to discredit these pat formulas about sheer will-power. Yet I do know a number of clinically depressed people aided by recent advances in antidepressant medication and by extended talking-therapy. It has been beneficial, too, for some clients and their families to read direct accounts by articulate depressives, portraying the numbness, disorientation, and despair that an outsider can scarcely imagine. At present no uniform explanation or solution for this affliction is certain. In fact, noting the common somatic features of depression, but its divergent psycho-social symptoms across cultures, many anthropologists even dispute its diagnosis as a single phenomenon.[15]

With the aid of every current therapeutic resource, the spiritually alert person will still try to handle this malaise somehow as a necessary pruning or weaning, a painful spiritual metamorphosis. Any hope that is coherent and practical may even spark the will to recovery. Chapter 4 described the mentally afflicted as those seeking for adequate metaphors to match an inner predicament. And each culture and religious tradition offers the flawed poet a specific range of images and symbolic behavior. Jung often found it useful to pull down a book from the shelf and show his client a fairy tale or biblical passage with archetypal motifs parallel to the disorder under treatment. By this process, he says, "the individual is lifted out of his miserable loneliness, and represented as undergoing a heroic meaningful fate which is ultimately good for the whole world, like the suffering and death of a god." A profound myth can "mobilize the forces of the unconscious to such an extent that even the nervous system becomes affected," and the body may begin to heal itself.[16]

Most Theravada Buddhists, for example, remember a touching parable in the Anguttara Commentary. This story has often lifted up an individual's unique grief or depression to a more universal solidarity in human misery. Kisa Gotami's only child dies, and in her uncontrollable mourning she is frantic to try any medicine for restoring the baby to life. The Buddha Gautama promises to restore her child if Kisa can bring the Buddha back a mustard seed from just one house where death has never occurred. Eagerly knocking at one door after another, she gradually opens herself with reluctance to the grief of others, and at last gives up the impossible quest. Transcending her own self-centered distress, Kisa returns enlightened to the Buddha. She crowns this nirvana experience with the decision to become a Buddhist nun.

Depression and mental suffering among Shiite Muslims can become for them, too, a uniquely religious experience. The tragic defeat of the House of Ali, especially the assassination of Muhammed's grandson Husayn and his family, has always touched the deepest Shiite feelings in Iran, Iraq, Pakistan, and India. By identifying with the Imam

Husayn's martyrdom at Karbala, the faithful Muslim realizes once again that the just must always suffer in an unjust world. Christians in a comparable way often interpret depression as a Dark Night ordeal, or more concretely, as a reenactment of Christ's agony in the garden or his crucifixion. In a letter I received a few years ago from prison, a devout Christian friend enclosed a rough pencil sketch of Jesus carrying his cross, the figure with whom this convict identifies at his own nadir of loneliness and humiliation. His caption borrows the words attributed in Mark's Gospel to Jesus on the cross, "God, my God, why have you abandoned me?" Asking me to pray for his patience, the letter closes with deep feeling: "My two hands are bleeding from the nails."

Meeting of the Three Ways

This is the last of three chapters exploring the Ways of Action, Affectivity, and Contemplation converging toward the sacred, and their innumerable counterfeits. In the familiar x-ray sketch of an ideal Hindu yogi, we find a classical embodiment of all three Ways. Tantric or Kundalini Yoga views the full-fledged Contemplative Way as a late developmental stage in yoga practice. You are asked to imagine sacred energy expanding in the body through consistent meditation and bodily exercises. It rises progressively through various chakras or gauges, activating the spinal column like a thermometer, from its base to a spiritual point above the head. As each dormant spiritual potential awakens, consciousness gradually shifts its center from the ego to the world, and finally to the sacred.

A beginner might fixate early in spiritual growth, for example, on material concerns or sexuality, symbolized by the anus and genitals. Some may soon reach the third chakra, located symbolically at the navel, center of ambition and the will to power. This level is a matrix for the Way of Action and its shortcomings. The fourth chakra, associated with the heart, offers a foundation for unselfish love and higher values—developmental roots for the Way of Affectivity. As energy ascends through the throat, eye, and brain skyward, the Way of Contemplation emerges, the first in many expanding phases of higher consciousness.[17]

This popular diagram has clear teaching advantages. First, by intertwining body and spirit, it avoids an ethereal spirituality, and especially a lopsided mind-body dichotomy. Second, by connecting all three Ways in a developmental sequence, it encourages each individual life to test out and combine all three. Third, it offers interesting parallels with the developmental psychology of Freud and Fromm. For example, shakti energy ascends like the progressive sublimation of libido. You catch echoes of the Freudian anal and genital phases, or Erich Fromm's distinction between the receptive infant, the exploitative marketing attitude of the child, and the active productive adult.

However, at one crucial point, this Tantric blueprint differs from the suppositions behind my present three chapters. It subordinates Action to Affectivity, and treats both as inferior to Contemplation. I think this just an elitist bias, commonplace to mystics of both East and West. According to my own conviction, on the contrary, spiritual Ways cannot be ranked. As emphasized before, no Way ought to be pursued in isolation from the other two. The Ways are simply three options, varying according to temperament, culture, particular religious custom, and individual experience. Any one Way, lived with balance or integrity, can serve as a comprehensive spirituality.

8

The Healing Spirit

One major premise in this book has been the continuity between sacred and profane, between the religious center of one's life and a mature personality. The present chapter shifts attention from various ways of healing, explored in earlier chapters, and now examines the healers themselves, immersed in this same sacred-profane dialectic.

As explained before, not everyone will accept my premise of continuity, especially when it is applied to the specialized healer. Many psychologists and therapists today view their profession as an impartial science, sanitized from contaminating religious influences. Freud, for instance, at various times in his career argued that psychoanalysis is neither a religious nor an anti-religious worldview, but a value-free method. He never questions the rationale commonly given for the birth of psychology and other modern sciences in Europe. According to this viewpoint, the enlightened mind gradually casts aside its earlier mystique of myth and woo-woo noises. Alchemy turns into chemistry, astrology into astronomy, traditional healing into pharmacy and medicine. In the same way, shamanic healers, succeeded by priest exorcists and spiritual directors, all at last yield their turf to the psychotherapist. Each phase is perceived uncritically as progress—increasing specialization, the triumph of creativity and reason, lopping off the barnacles of superstition.

An ironic summary of this advance is offered by the main character in *Roger's Version*, a novel by John Updike: "Whenever theology touches science, it gets burned. In the sixteenth century astronomy, in the seventeenth microbiology, in the eighteenth geology and paleontology, in the nineteenth Darwin's biology all grotesquely extended the world-frame and sent churchmen scurrying for cover in ever smaller, more shadowy nooks, little gloomy ambiguous caves in the psyche where even now neurology is cruelly harrying them, gouging them out from the multifolded brain like wood lice from under the lumber pile."[1]

Yet this myth of scientific advance clearly satisfies just a single culture and era. Most non-European societies, and especially the Primal traditions, have seldom isolated the functions of shaman, priest, and therapist. They view these roles, not in progressive sequence, but in juxtaposition or fusion. African Primal cultures, for example, usually treat the *nganga* or shaman as an unbounded spiritual and therapeutic factotum, to be consulted for healing an illness, passing a driver's test, communicating with an ancestor, detecting or preventing a crime.[2]

Even in America at the beginning of this century, William James would have felt more affinity with an American Indian shaman than with Freud's value-free psychoanalyst. The audience that listened to James' *Varieties of Religious Experience* lectures in 1902 had experienced a flood of spiritual-therapeutic movements, such as traditional herbal healing, Mesmerism, Theosophy, Christian Science, and hydropathic and homeopathic magic. Today, since the counter-culture of the sixties, we have been rediscovering this rich holistic pre-Freudian milieu. Some recent consumers' guides to therapy introduce psychoanalysis as just one of many viable therapies. There are chapters, too, on Rolfing, sex therapy, primal scream, Zen, stress management, hypnotherapy, Christotherapy, organic foods, biofeedback, and transcendental meditation.

The blending of both religious and therapeutic roles can be illustrated by a resourceful Taiwanese student of mine. A few years ago Linlee asked me for a bottle of Catholic holy water, which she intended for exorcising evil spirits from her friend Hoong's apartment. Distraught for some months by eerie sounds, misplaced furniture, and nightmares, Hoong had tried various unsuccessful Taoist charms and incantations. Hoong was Buddhist, Linlee a Methodist. Now my own temperament, training, and faith, as explained in chapter 3, prompt me to check the underside in tales of ghosts and demons, and never to let prayer be mistaken for magic. Thus, probing for details of Hoong's homesickness and depression, I hoped to deflect Linlee's attention from unappeased ghosts to her friend's own emotional disturbance. Perhaps Hoong needed counseling, either from Linlee or a specialist.

Partial to my suggestions, Linlee began to rehearse a number of practical ways to ease her friend's loneliness. If Hoong's belief in ghosts should persist, Linlee agreed to share a few of her own impromptu prayers for God's protection, rather than snatch at holy water, a Catholic symbol uncongenial to her own Methodist background. She left, apparently eager to try out her redefined mission. A few weeks later, however, I ran into Linlee, and discovered she had given my own redirecting efforts a further ironic quarter-turn. She had tiptoed into a Catholic church, boldly scooped a container of holy water from the entrance font, and devised her own creative rite with candles, incense, and water to exorcise the haunted apartment. For she sensed that Hoong would never accept Linlee's role as peer counselor until Hoong had been overawed by her friend's convincing performance as exorcist, with all the gothic props.

As trained professionals, both the priest and the therapist might be wary of a woman like Linlee—an amateur, perhaps a harmful quack, trampling the neat fences between highly specialized roles. Yet the culture and temperament of Hoong would probably have barred her direct consultation with either specialist. More important, Linlee herself most likely represents a talented mix of the religious and therapeutic.

By examining these two distinct but correlated healing roles more carefully, the present chapter will test out the implications of their conflict, fusion, or precarious alliance. It locates the marrow of genuine healing authority and empathy, and attempts to distinguish it from religious and psychological counterfeits.

The Therapist as Guru

As an inclusive context for therapy, you are asked to imagine, not a clinic or private carpeted office, but a room in someone's home, perhaps with a small area set aside for receiving visitors. The place could be a shaman's hut, or even the crowded study at Freud's Vienna residence, centering on the original psychoanalytic couch. The therapy situation I have in mind matches that described in "The Prophetess," a short story by Njabulo Ndebele of South Africa.[3] Though a few narrative details look similar to the improvised exorcism recounted above, Ndebele's tale has its own insightful psychology and spirituality.

With obvious mythical overtones of the epic quest and adolescent rites of passage, this story traces a boy's arduous mission to fetch water blessed by a local prophetess to heal his sick mother. Unfortunately, the bottle containing her cure smashes during the final lap of his journey back from the home of the prophetess. Unready to repeat his quest or come home defeated, however, the boy replaces it with a bottle of ordinary tap water, which manages to bring relief somehow to his mother.

The boy does not relish any pretense or irony in his final strategy. At first he feels horror at the possible taboos violated by counterfeit holy water. But awareness comes gradually. The prophetess herself, in words he could not comprehend at the time, had redefined his original mission, and now at his mother's bedside, he senses in himself the presence of the sacred. "He had the power of the prophetess in him. And he was going to pass that power to his mother, and heal her." His guilt and fear at last vanish. "There was such a glow of warmth in the boy as he watched his mother, so much gladness in him, that he forgave himself."

Through his encounter with the sacred healer, this boy has had a momentous initiatory experience—both therapeutic and spiritual. At the shrine of the prophetess, he had entered as just a stand-in or go-between. Yet he went away healed, and more important, a healer. What occurred was an expansion and gestalt shift in consciousness, what theologians call a hermeneutical reversal. The sacred here, or in any of its manifestations elsewhere, is not to be judged, but stands in judgment. It is not chosen but does the choosing. Your first impulse may be to trim this profound encounter down to size, so that it can fit easy familiar categories. Yet resisting your interpretation, and rearranging your unconscious agenda, it most of all reinterprets you to yourself. You may come as a mere passenger or observer, but you cannot leave untouched. Brushing aside your agenda, the sacred text, rite, or person sounds this challenge: how are your spiritual horizons affected now by a fresh heightened realization of what it means to hope, love, or die?

A similar reversal occurs in any psychotherapy that involves a true in-depth relationship. As mentioned in chapter 4, Freud laments the shallow and often misleading situations presented for routine psychoanalysis. Parents want the analyst to treat a daughter considered unruly, just because she disobeys their selfish, damaging injunctions. Or a husband forces his nervous wife into treatment to save a marriage that depends on her neurosis for its very existence. But the analyst in conscience cannot bring about the results demanded. For the presenting problem itself may prove "incompatible with the conditions necessary for psychoanalysis." Freud intends to smoke out such an incompatibility from the start. Otherwise, therapy would be comparable to working under a prospective house-owner "who orders an architect to build him a villa according to his own tastes and requirements, or of a pious donor who commissions an artist to paint a sacred picture in the corner of which is to be a portrait of himself in adoration."[4]

From his perspective four decades later, Erich Fromm surmises that clients usually approached Freud as they would a conventional physician, with complaints of easily labeled disorders, such as an hysteric paralysis or a washing compulsion. The cure they sought corresponded to their concept of sickness—removal of specific symptoms. Clients of our own era, on the other hand, though focusing initially on some particular complaint, are better disposed than their forerunners to recognize vast spiritual upheaval underneath. Fromm is convinced the real problem for people today is not depression, insomnia, their marriage, or their job. Such complaints are only the conscious form in which your own society permits you to hint at something much deeper. You feel outraged that wealth has not brought happiness, frightened that life may give out before you have truly lived, alienated from nature and others and even your own self.[5]

Thus Freud and Fromm do not hesitate to redefine the basis and scope of their client's presenting problem. They find mere adjustment therapy intolerable. For it just tames and reinserts the victim back into a disordered family or society. Therapists themselves are expected to discriminate between genuine and counterfeit values, both in individuals and civilizations. Only then can the client be reintroduced into society, either to reaffirm the world or to change it. *Secular pastoral worker* is the hesitant term Freud in his later career applies to the analyst's role—not reclaiming souls for the Church, but restoring persons to the human community.

In a similar way, the prophetess in Ndebele's story is intent on redirecting the boy's initial self-perception as a neutral emissary, insulated from healing. "What did you say you wanted, little man?" she asks the frightened boy. He identifies his mother as a staff nurse, and then requests the water needed. In an exchange reminiscent of the Gospel dialogue between Jesus and Nicodemus, playing on some confusion between ordinary water and healing water of the Spirit, the woman tries to help this young messenger sense the religious implications of his mission. "You see, you should learn to say what you mean," she says. Commending his mother's widely known generosity, and the boy's care for her, the prophetess urges him to learn and serve, but especially to "listen to new things. Then try to create, too." She blesses the water with her bamboo cross, and begs God for rebirth and fertility. After asking the boy to kneel, she places her hands on his head, searching around the scalp and down his neck, so that he can actually feel "the soul of the prophetess going into him." Then she sends him home to heal.

Thus both charism and advice from the therapist have been transformed into a healing force inherent to the client. And an essential ingredient in this and any other cure is the capacity to extend it to others. The model therapy situation in this story has underscored the presence of a pervasive moral or spiritual component. This latter dimension, however, is either magnified or overlooked in the two imbalances that will now be examined.

The Inflated Guru

The inflated guru is a person cultivating an aura of omniscience and inaccessibility. Judging this sort of attitude one of the major hazards in his profession, Freud compares this work to that of an x-ray technician handling radioactive matter. "It would not be surprising if the effect of a constant preoccupation with all the repressed material which struggles for freedom in the human mind were to stir up in analysts as well all the instinctual demands they are otherwise able to keep under suppression." Especially deceptive are the heavy transference projections that arise in almost every therapy relationship. To guard against contamination, Freud advises even veteran analysts to receive a *nachanalyse* or recurrent training analysis, at least every five years.[6]

It is plausible that the average healer will prove vulnerable to fantasies of self-importance. The work commonly occurs in unvaried isolation, seated for hours a day, focused mostly on a clientele very limited in number, social class, and ideas. The alleged rate of depression and suicide in the therapy profession is ominous. As a trained listener, you do not get many opportunities to share your own spontaneous opinions and inner life. Yet one way to compensate for boredom or despair is to savor the uncritical appreciation expressed by those you have helped. Soon this adulation tempts you to range beyond limited professional competence. You show up on media interviews to chart the profile of a hunted psychopath, or advise those coping with an earthquake disaster, or analyze the foibles of strangers with political and religious views at variance with your own.[7]

In this therapeutic age, insecure counselors at times display their analytic skill as an armor of superiority, threatening and manipulative. For example, the short story "Age of Analysis" by Lynne Schwartz fixes on the consciousness of Paul, a disturbed adolescent son of two therapists headed for divorce. It is ridiculous that Paul and his parents must consult their own three separate therapists to help each family member deal with the other two.

All the therapists in this story, including Paul's parents, hide genuine feelings under a veneer of psychobabble. Even while Paul rages at his new therapist, she smiles and reaches for her appointment book, indicating their fifty minute session is over. "If I gave you the sympathy you want, it wouldn't help the treatment. I understand how you feel—we'll have to deal with that, too." And when Paul shrieks and destroys furniture to get through to his father, the man just urges him to relay this anger to the boy's therapist. "You think I'm a bastard, fine, tell her. Say anything. She'll help you deal with it." Paul finds the game rules of "dealing with" an evasive fraud. Each attitude becomes just a way of dealing with endless geological layers of attitudes beneath.[8]

The sharpest critique of deified analysts can be found in Jung, who himself knew how it felt to be adored by a circle of Valkyries. Most clients yearn to locate a savior, and will meet little resistance persuading the therapist to endorse their predictable choice. Analysts of this sort begin to make themselves a nuisance at medical conventions, but gradually become more exclusive and solitary. The moment they feel "equal to the mahatmas in the Himalayas," you know they are lost to the profession. "They could not resist the continuous onslaught of the patients' collective unconscious—case after case projecting the savior complex and religious expectations. . . . They identify with the archetype, they discover a creed of their own, and since they need disciples who believe in them, they will found a sect."[9]

Jung implies that once Eurocentric analysts aspire to the attributes of a conventional Hindu guru, they have already become deracinated and fraudulent. Yet taking a more generous view of Hindu belief, you can find wisdom there that bridges most cultural boundaries. Any qualified Hindu chosen to impart knowledge of the self is esteemed more highly in this tradition than even one's own mother and father. "For while parents give a physical body," say the ancient Laws of Manu, a guru "gives the spiritual, eternal body." Moreover, for those Hindus believing that all reality is Brahman or exists in Brahman, the guru becomes second to God or a "second God." As an insightful corollary to this belief, in some ashram initiation rites, the guru kneels before each prepared candidate, and tells the disciple, "Now you have become a god, and now I am worshiping you."

Nevertheless, many discerning Hindus are anxious to repudiate any hint of idolatry toward the guru figure. It has been observed that most people want to be a guru, but no one a disciple. One swami offers a marvelous excuse for celebrating his guru's feast day. After this particular saint once refused to become his guru, the swami began to learn for himself. In other words, what commonly begins as a guru-force in your mentor or therapist must at last become your own inherent guide. The Tantric Buddhist guru tradition, too, urges this same process of guru-internalization. Similar to the mounting transference relationship and its resolution in formal therapy, your relationship to the guru advances from a honeymoon or personality cult, to a final moment, when this particular mentor means no more to you than a dog or rock by the wayside. Eventually you see the "guru-quality" in each life situation, and "all things can become the guru."[10]

The Uncommitted Guru

Here an immediate paradox arises. The above discussion commended the genuine self-acknowledged guru, who by an act of will is transformed into an inner healing force within the client. Yet now, on the contrary, an even more self-effacing sort of healer will be called into question. This is the crypto-guru, allegedly uncommitted or neutral, with no acknowledged moral or religious function.

There are religious thinkers, of course, who disdain the findings and methods of psychology. Just as those who slight history are condemned to repeat it, so theologians of this sort are condemned to draw upon their own unconscious psychology of fallacious common sense. In a comparable way, therapists insulated from serious constructive thought about ethics, political realities, and religious life, will usually be guided by their own muddled intuition on these matters. Left unconscious, these opinions and attitudes will seep irresponsibly into the therapy process, to its detriment.

Thus, addressing the intricate issues of life that surface in counseling, and supporting an implicit religious worldview, therapists often seem half-aware or ignorant of their actual guru function. In my conscientious objector advising during the sixties, for example, I could have provided the names of psychiatrists certain to sign a medical exemption form. They did this not for money, but from what I gathered were implicit political and moral sympathies against the war. Yet their conscious diagnosis fell back on the language of dispassionate clinical objectivity.

A startling example of god-like analytical neutrality can be found in the scenario imagined by Abbot Gregorio Lemercier, head of the famous Benedictine monastery in Cuernavaca, Mexico, during the sixties. After completing a successful Freudian analysis under Dr. Quevedo, the abbot could not wait until his religious community experienced a comparable awakening. The individual and group analyses that ensued at Cuernavaca had their counterpart among priests and sisters during this same decade in the United States—sensitivity training or T-groups of various types, often compulsory in a particular religious group, or a prerequisite for many Catholic institutes in pastoral counseling. At any rate, after less than one year's psychoanalysis, more than half the Cuernavaca monastery was emptied. Many in the community, according to their abbot, proved afraid "to confront their own essential selves."

It is unfortunate that Lemercier provides no evidence whether these monks at last found their true vocations outside the monastery, or if the quality of religious commitment later improved inside. But the remaining members voted eventually to drop their monastic affiliation and become instead a therapy-oriented group of lay people. Lemercier's revised dream now called for a "humanly ecumenical" community of Communist, Catholic, Lutheran, Buddhist, Mormon men and women. They would be united, no longer merely to share religious ideas, but to analyze feelings without prejudice. To direct them, the group would choose a psychoanalyst, qualified as "just an analyst," and not of any particular religious persuasion. Here Lemercier commits himself not merely to the therapeutic ideal, but to psychoanalysis alone, just one particular filament in the web of contemporary therapies. And he trusts the psychoanalyst almost unconditionally, just as analyst. By definition the fallible human figure cast in this leadership role is expected to transcend all religious or moral particularity.[11]

Freud and Jung were both cited before, alarmed at the snares set by client devotees. An even greater hazard for the contemporary therapist is an eagerness in church people like Lemercier to sit at the therapist's feet. History has demonstrated the closed disdain shown by many religious authorities to any unsettling new discoveries. Also, after being trained so long to generate answers, veteran theologians often cannot hear the actual questions raised by specialists from another discipline. Yet in this current Age of the Therapeutic, on the contrary, you will overhear preachers of all faiths addressing their congregation about the mid-life crisis, peak-experiences, and phases of moral development. Self-help therapists are cited as oracles on how to love or believe, and even how to die. Thus, if psychologists expect to remain alert and modest today, they could use a bracing dialogue with the serious religious critic, not just with some docile clerical disciple.

Maslow, Carl Rogers, and other Humanistic Psychologists, for instance, offer an idealistic cure marked by attitudes of unconditional regard, self-esteem, or "I'm okay." Yet this position is based on an implicit religious premise about the utopian capacities in human nature. From my own standpoint I would argue that unlimited self-actualization is neither possible nor desirable. Distorted lives can stem from too little self-esteem, but also from too much. An actualized individual requires the counterbalance of mature self-restriction. I also challenge the presumption that two self-actualized individuals can never thwart each other, or that individual self-interest will automatically benefit everyone else in shaping a utopian community. Such a dream gives no hint of the ambiguities and collisions that life has taught most of us to expect even when relatively mature, well-motivated individuals try to share the same bathroom or meeting hall.[12]

I am convinced that every therapy, even psychoanalysis in its purest form, can never be value-free in actual practice. As mentioned before, Freud presumes some ethical basis for challenging particular family or social beliefs prevalent among his clients. Even his analytical couch tradition has left its impact on values. For example, in Persian miniatures you can observe the insertion of a blinding flame or faceless blank to represent Muhammed's presence, just as early Buddhist art usually wipes out the figure of the Buddha Gautama in a group scene. Though the original purpose of this artistic convention was to avoid idolatry, its effect is often just the opposite—a sacred apophatic silence. In a comparable manner, the unseen therapist looming behind a couch, with heightened aesthetic distance, can elicit transference reactions close to religious worship. Moreover, the very decor and furniture selected for an office, the way analysts dress and talk, their chosen titles, the disclosures they decide to respond or not respond to, their interpretations of what is functional or dysfunctional—these signals and many others communicate their private spiritual and moral worldview to the client.

Yet at its best, Freud's style of therapy offers a context of strict confidentiality and honesty, conducive to an uninhibited "free association" of feelings. Lifting the filter of social and personal censorship, clients promise to relax and express their most forbidden fantasies. What emerge at last are the values unconsciously guiding their past, with an added privilege now of reassessing this moral inheritance from family, church, society, and other sources. Bringing these values to consciousness might seem at first a mere prelude to ethics, a propaideutic. But a sigh, smile, or shrug from the analyst at this moment could have massive influence. And there are surely some authoritarian believers whose faith could never survive this unaccustomed exposure to free inquiry, free speech, and a demand for persuasive coherence.

Many people throughout life, and especially in moments of crisis, seek the ideal place, time, and guide for a spiritual reprieve. This must prove a sanctuary of acceptance and support, in which they can examine their accustomed self-image, test out new images of themselves and others, and perhaps initiate a transformation. The ritual setting may be a retreat house, ashram, or clinic. It may even mean a Freudian oasis of candid free association for a few hours each week. Once clients become aware of their own value system, they have already taken the first step toward release from its unconscious bondage. But after that moment, each individual has yet to begin testing out and reconstructing a more mature ethics, deciding what to reaffirm, discard, or transform from before.

Whereas clients need to clarify and reaffirm their own center of religious meaning, they have the right to count on a reciprocal gesture from the mature therapist—a continuous process that someone has called axio-analysis. This is an evolving awareness and self-criticism of one's own religious premises, especially their impact on the handling of particular cases. No training analysis makes sense without this dimension, which includes a lifelong supervision and consultation with colleagues. Watchers need to be watched, and analysts analyzed, especially for protection against the ever underestimated hazards of transference.[13]

Empathy and Its Facsimiles

Ndebele's story of the prophetess, recounted earlier in this chapter, spends a full quarter of its narrative on the boy's reluctant, shuddering approach to her house. His mind is swirling with rumors about her moods, unavailability, and sorcery. But what makes her surprisingly approachable, once he enters, is the smell of camphor on her body. His mother always used camphor for rheumatism. Was the prophetess ill then? Perhaps this strange woman had to bless holy water for curing her own disorders. "Suddenly, the boy felt at ease, as if the discovery that a prophetess could also feel pain somehow made her explainable." In other words, the boy's recognition of a shared mortality lessens the staggering aesthetic distance, the exaggerated tremors of awe and mystery. Without this moment, he could not have entrusted himself later to the prophetess, when she breathed her spirit into his own at the climax of their healing experience.

Both the healer and the healed peer into each other's eyes, and recognize each in the other. During my own early adolescence, I once fretted and delayed, no less fearful than Ndebele's fictional character, and finally broached an anonymous priest concealed in the dark confessional box. I shall never forget the warm assurance that took me by surprise: "Don't be afraid. I'm no judge, but your brother. A sinner just like you!" This theme of the wounded healer, or the healing glance of shared recognition, occurs in most shamanic healings throughout the Primal traditions. In some societies, shaman candidates are qualified by the presence of sickness, mental disturbance, or near-death moments in their own past, all implying privileged intimacy with spiritual frontiers. According to one popular explanation for their therapeutic success, shamans during each dramatic cure reenact the agony of their own original illness. They introduce it into the patient's consciousness as a persuasive new explanatory vision.

These illustrations all suggest the conditions and outcome of *empathy*. The term means literally the ability to feel into, or feel inside, another situation. Few know better what this process implies than the great lyric poets. Gerard Manley Hopkins talks of *inscape*, and John Keats of annihilating his very self and "entering into" the natural world around him. Rilke's famous notion of *einsehen* or in-seeing comes closest to my own position. By merely inspecting a dog, for example, Rilke might pass through the dog itself and out the other side into its human meaning. But by in-seeing, he lets himself into the dog's very center, the point where it begins to be a dog, where God has just created it, knew that it was good, and that it could not have been better made.[14]

Thus, feeling-into the life of others, you enter into their world and worldview, and try to feel, value, and believe as they do. This Coleridgean "willing suspension of disbelief"—or more accurately, the partial soft-pedaling of your own individual belief—is not too difficult if you and the others share the same reassuring background. However, the more you diverge from another person in language, temperament, and religious tradition, the more obstacles you must remove for an eager foray into regions of the truly other.

A striking instance of the unexplored barriers to empathy once emerged during my course in Asian religious traditions. A forty-year-old veteran of the Vietnamese War, who wore a large cross around his neck, showed initial enthusiasm for the lectures. But later he ceased attending. Eventually tracking me down to explain his reasons for dropping the class, he made a remarkable disclosure, which I have never forgotten. Too many torments of his past had been churned up by the class discussions and films. It now occurred to him that he had often killed in combat, solaced by an image of God fighting alongside him against a godless enemy. Yet he was now recognizing for the first time that the enemy might be individual Buddhists, Taoists, or worse, Asian fellow Christians, all perhaps no less religious than he. The man was not yet ready to work out the horrifying implications of this self-deception.

Careful use of the word empathy emphasizes a specific sort of relationship. First, it intends to avoid the demeaning overtones often attached to misunderstood gestures of pity, sympathy, and compassion. More important, this attitude does not mean sheer identification or projection, but a context of balanced participation and observation. As a young high school teacher, for instance, I was exhorted repeatedly, "Don't teach the subject, teach students." Yet at the same time veteran teachers cautioned, "Don't smile until Christmas," and "Try too hard to be their friend, and you'll lose their respect." In other words, one must be able simultaneously to experience intensely with, and think critically about, other people.

The excessive observer is remote and impersonal, unable to taste the marrow of life from the inside. The excessive participant, however, is immersed mind and heart in some situation, but also enmeshed in it, and therefore stripped of a privileged outside perspective. Thus, a balanced therapist must oscillate with care between both polarities of disengagement and engagement. This dialectic combines what Alfred North Whitehead calls the moments of precision and of romance. Expressed more precisely, the therapist-observer enlists the client-observer to interpret what both of them experience as mutual participants in therapy.

Cautioning against an excessive observer-mode, even Freud prefers a "cordial human relationship" with clients. He is convinced the therapist with exaggerated analytic passivity "spoils the effect of analysis by a certain listless indifference, and then neglects to lay bare the resistances which he thereby awakens in his patient."[15] This very deficiency gradually revealed itself during my own counseling apprenticeship. One day a sudden phone call interrupted a client interview in my office. On the line was a friend with whom I had lost touch many years before. Talking within inches of the client's face, I must have shown great affection and delight at this surprising voice on the phone, before I took her number for a later call. As I resumed our therapy session, the client seated before me was candid enough to point up the contrast between my obvious warmth on the phone, and the disciplined, resolutely genteel voice of the professional therapist.

At the opposite extremity, you will find some therapists almost engulfed in a folie à deux relationship. The analyst Robert Lindner tells about the "Case of the Jet-Propelled Couch," in which his gifted client had conjured up a very detailed, coherent escape-fantasy on another planet, a friendlier and more exciting realm than this man's routine research work. To gain rapport with an otherwise unreachable client, Lindner gradually familiarizes himself with the secret language of this realm, imagines himself an inhabitant there, and before he can stop himself, fixates on its beauty, from which he cannot extricate himself. Their sessions soon consist of such topics as "How are things in Seraneb? How goes it with the Chystopeds?" At their final interview, the client admits having freed himself from his fantasy. However he did sustain a pretended belief in it through some months, just to avoid hurting Lindner, who obviously needed the fantasy more than he.[16]

One purpose for the therapist's ongoing self-therapy is to help discern true empathy from its misleading facsimiles. For example, one client may tell you of a traumatic mugging incident, with which you can readily identify as her therapist, because you, too, were once beaten in similar circumstances as a child. While listening to her story, perhaps you replay your own past experience, so that as a result you may even edit out some details, and plug apparent gaps in her account. These engaged attitudes filter and heighten your direct perception of the present narrative. Unless you separate your own unique memories from the client's account, she could be reduced to a mere projection of your own.

It is possible to experience empathy, and yet lack the communicative skills to manifest it. On the other hand, its expression may have to be redirected or withheld for wise therapeutic reasons. For example, at my supervisor's request, I once played my tape from a sample counseling session, recorded with the client's permission. We listened to the refined, anxious voice of a young divorcee: "At times I don't know where to turn. I feel panic. I almost think I'm going out of my mind." She followed this remark with a timid giggle. Then you could hear the ridiculous antiphonal burst of my own laughter.

Stopping the recording, and replaying it a few times, the supervisor pressed me to explain why I laughed at that moment, what I actually felt, and what I could now conjecture had been communicated by my laugh. "Empathy," I claimed defensively, "Unconditional regard, support, encouragement." But the man suggested otherwise. I was feeling panic at the fear this woman had expressed about losing her mind. And my laugh was a way to cover up my own panic, the very defense she was using to disguise hers. Worst of all, the therapeutic effect of my own laughter was to bolster her defensive maneuver, yet keep her from touching upon her fright underneath it. A disciplined empathy ought to focus on her panic, not her evasion. "How awful it must be," I should have commented, "to feel you're losing your mind!"

Again, based on genuine empathy I might judge it necessary to hospitalize people endangering themselves or others, or intervene in some other way that strikes clients as unempathic or rejecting. At any rate, in all these complex situations, I think it essential first to feel actual empathy, and not fabricate its presence. Throughout my own training as therapist, however, too many of us lost ourselves in the sheer techniques of communicating it.[17] We learned suitable greetings, handshakes or hugs, gestures of sitting close, leaning forward with intent, or nodding and uttering an affirmative "ummh!" This stylized bedside manner also featured a new grammar—bland and circumlocutory, favoring the subjunctive or optative mode, in interventions like this: "I hear you saying you would find it inappropriate to continue." This billowing rhetoric aims to elicit genuine feelings from the client, without prompting an expected response or projecting your own.

Conclusion: A Healing Empathy

Some people find no trace of empathy in their bones. But others seem to have entered life with a temperament and imagination almost preternaturally empathic. For me, this capacity has always seemed a charism or grace, an implicit experience of the sacred. It has the power to heal both the person feeling it and the person toward whom it is felt. It cannot be willed, but shows up in a flash of serendipity. Though often momentary, the privilege to transcend one's own egocentric boundaries must never be taken for granted.

Even for those with a tenuous hold on this gift, there are ways to nourish it more actively. Granted that books cannot replace actual life, many classics of fiction and biography do enhance the scope of empathy. Testing and stretching the limited imagination, they help train a third ear, able to detect the extraordinary inner life of ordinary people. What at first seems repelling about Joe Christmas or Raskolnikov in the novels of Faulkner and Dostoevsky, for example, is now gradually uncovered as their bewildered pain, the compulsions and fears that might drive almost anyone to violence and death. More fair than most other writers to criminals and sinners, Dostoevsky also shows a shrewd dramatic flair in placing some of his most intense private convictions on the lips of those characters with whom you would expect him to disagree.

A recent disclosure by novelist William Styron indicates the vast empathic range of an artist's creative unconscious. From the quicksand of his own clinical depression, hospitalization, and near-suicide, Styron says he would page through sequences from his earlier novels, written before he had any hints of his approaching disorder. He was stunned to perceive how accurately he had created the landscape of depression and psychic imbalance that led one young heroine after another to destruction. "Thus depression, when it finally came to me, was in fact no stranger, not even a visitor totally unannounced. It had been tapping at my door for decades."[18] When discussing serious disorders in chapter 4, I commended the respect shown by most therapists for the emotional logic of mad dreams, hallucinations, and irrational behavior. Thus, whenever you vicariously "feel inside" a disturbed client or the imagined character from a novel, you acknowledge implicitly that this suffering or deviance has long been no stranger to your own unconscious life.

In my own counseling, a number of bracing experiences through the years have apparently strengthened my own ability to empathize, though the feeling still at times deserts me. Each of these situations overtook me by surprise, and turned into a providential chance to learn. During a few years of part-time hospital chaplaincy, for example, I often yearned to reach out more earnestly toward some of the dying or very sick people I had come to know. When words seemed to falter between us, a friendly touch on the arm or shoulder had to suffice—an empathic gesture that seemed effective because it leaped intuitively from my own need. I met comparable opportunities during the summer of 1975 in Guam working with Vietnamese refugees fleeing Saigon, or four months in Nepal, where each day I visited residents and outpatients in my Jesuit friend's overcrowded drug rehabilitation center.

At this Kathmandu clinic, treatments consisted mostly of acupuncture, administered to the earlobes, apparently triggering opiate receptors in the brain to contrive a sort of methadone facsimile. Unable to speak much Nepali, I tried to reach beyond words, and recognize profound feelings of hunger, fear, or love, which no language in the world could register anyway. I often played volleyball with the residents and outpatients, or sat nearby with a reassuring smile as they awaited their daily needles. My animated pantomime and grin, seldom apparent back home, now flourished to make up for a crippling aphasia. And this smile, in turn, seemed to evoke similar smiles in those I met, so that I both projected and welcomed back a more congenial ambiance than is customary with me. Again, during a few months as chaplain at a Vietnamese refugee camp in Guam, I was eager to reassure various distressed people through the limited English vocabulary we shared—crucial words like death, love, work, God, hope. I would drift from one group to another, sharing in their meals, witnessing incomprehensible card games, relying at times on translators for help in a particular counseling situation.

In both Guam and Nepal, though limited to a few words, I could at least offer a handshake, hug, or devout *namaste* greeting, with hands steepled before the lips. Perhaps I was edging unaware toward the transcultural gestures of a traditional Hindu guru, whose very openness to *darshan,* the locking of glances between guru and disciple, carries a promise of affectionate healing and a blessing.

One common feature emerges in these moments of empathic communication. Though entering the situation at first in a helping capacity, only gradually do I tend to recognize my own need, too, for help. Anthropologists in prolonged fieldwork describe at times a state of culture-shock, disorientation, regression, loneliness, paranoid fantasies, and mourning over the loss of one's own culture. This was surely my experience, too, during months of living with insiders in places like Germany, Japan, Thailand, rural Wales, and especially Nepal.

To make sense of unfamiliar contexts like these, it is helpful to expand the concept of transference and countertransference beyond the margins of formal therapy. Both terms would mean an unconscious projection of fantasies and feelings from one's past into the present experience. Often some intense new encounter in an alien culture may stir up memories that usually remain dormant back home. By disciplined reflection on these moments of countertransference, I have learned to pick up emotionally toned aspects about other people and our relationships that I ordinarily overlook.[19]

The director Peter Brook tells of blank masks he often urges his cast to wear during rehearsals. Liberated for a time from their subjectivity, actors often approach a role with new insight, and by withdrawing attention from the face, gain heightened awareness of their whole body. Perhaps almost everyone, especially a person of my own temperament and background, needs first to be stripped of habitual mental and verbal dodges, the insulation of defined roles. Once convinced of utter vulnerability, you can then fall back on the more chthonic resources of empathy. No longer identified with just the usual conventional self, you discover how to regress effectively. Perhaps you can now risk an exploration into other possible selves, both within and outside yourself.

The gift of empathy shows marked parallels with any generous attempt at religious tolerance or inclusiveness. As friendships with people of other faiths deepen, we tend to center more on the religious premises that unite us both—a quest for the Absolute, training in meditation under a guru or spiritual director, the need to redress common social injustices in our respective societies. It is not easy to open oneself to the faith and culture of another as truly other. Yet one sound motive for doing so is a feeling of empathy and friendship first for this actual individual. Then affection will nourish an eagerness to hear out and respect the most cherished convictions of that person. In my own counseling or teaching, for example, I have often stalled before some apparent fallacy or incoherence, say, in the Buddhist or Muslim faith. But then my imaginative empathy has been revived again and again by this rigorous litmus test: how would devout, informed friends like Kazu, Linlee, or Achmad have lived out this paradox and made sense of it?

One recurring motif of this book has been a needed inclusion and balance, especially in attempts to map out the converging three spiritual Ways of Action, Affectivity, and Contemplation. Chapter 5 has indicated how a myopic activism can shape the huckster televangelist, the Armageddon politician, or the Grand Inquisitor. The unbalanced affectivity analyzed in chapter 6 helps account for infatuation and self-laceration in cult devotees and anorexic saints. And as chapter 7 suggests, too rarefield a contemplative milieu breeds the misanthropic swami on a bed of nails, or the spiritual gourmet, scrounging for peak experiences. In other words, distortion or immaturity will always be associated with the one-sided and single-minded.

Following a similar pattern, my own source of empathy seems to drain away whenever I try to distill the essence exclusively of a trained analyst, and let it monitor my relations with actual people. At such moments, predictable counterfeits begin to surface. Action gets too manipulative, affectively turns either metallic or maudlin, and contemplation smothers on its own monoxide. On the other hand, my training in empathy has usually taken place beyond the strict therapeutic alliance, in situations where I was perceived not only as counselor, but also teacher, mentor, priest, and friend, often among people of the most varied cultures.

This same appreciation for a humane, flexible professional role marks the later career of Margaret Mead. In her autobiography, *Blackberry Winter*, she records a previous concern that becoming a mother and grandmother might compromise her trained nonpartisan viewpoint as an anthropologist. How could a mother avoid measuring each new child as younger, bigger, more or less graceful, intelligent, or skilled than her own child? Yet the marvel of actual motherhood proved otherwise. Years later, contemplating her two-year-old granddaughter, Mead could now observe the children around her with greater clarity—the meaning of puckered eyebrows, a tensed hand, the tongue groping for its first words. ''Instead of a bias that must be compensated for,'' she concludes, ''I have acquired a special and perhaps transient sensitivity. It is as if the child to whom one is bound by greater knowledge and the particularity of love were illuminated and carried a halo of light into any group of children.'' By now she had developed a more complete perspective, ''not as a professional student of childhood but simply as a human being.''[20]

Throughout these pages, my own detailed counseling memories have often implied a creative mix of roles—now teaching, coaching, praying beside, or engaging in mutual research with a client. This impulse to juxtapose and reconcile the otherwise fragmented comes as expected. For according to my basic premise in chapter 1, religious growth and psychological growth are distinct but inseparable components, each needing the other for an integral human life.

Another major premise, developed in chapters 4 and 7, endorses the Way of Action, or Affectivity, or Contemplation as a single comprehensive spirituality, provided that it is lived with balance or integrity. In a comparable interaction no less crucial, the priest, the therapist, and the guru or shaman represent three distinct vocations. Each is marked by a different specialized training, with its own respected history and certification. The ideal healer must begin someplace concretely—settle on just one of these three roles, and then spend a lifetime trying to embody it inclusively.

Carl Jung always defined the art of psychotherapy as part of a broader cure of souls. "Neurosis is not a thing apart but the whole of a pathologically disturbed psyche . . . What matters is not the neurosis, but the person who has a neurosis." Jung hoped to train a new species of therapist, heir to the alchemist and medical philosopher of a distant past, when body and soul, psychology and religion, had not yet been split into different domains of specialization. "Although we are specialists par excellence, our specialized field, oddly enough, drives us to universalism and to the complete overcoming of the specialist attitude, if the totality of body and soul is not just to be a matter of words."[21]

Thus, the distinct traditions of analysis, spiritual direction, and shamanic cure converge whenever someone strives to heal, not just as a specialist, but as a complete human being. What distinguishes one particular healer from another is less important than the common vision that unites them. At best, they share a comprehensive healing ideal, wide enough to interweave every possible source of insight and care.

Notes

Chapter 1. Sacred Disguises: The Alias and the Counterfeit *(pp. 1–12)*

1. See discussion of the religious adjective in Wilfred Cantwell Smith, "Secularity and the History of Religions," *The Spirit and Power of Christian Secularity*, ed. Albert Schlitzer, C.S.C. (Notre Dame: University of Notre Dame Press, 1969) 33–58. This pervasive concept is applied to the study of Primal religious traditions in Kenelm Burridge, *Encountering Aborigines: A Case Study* (New York: Pergamon Press, 1973) 169ff.

2. Georg Simmel, "A Contribution to the Sociology of Religion," tr. W. W. Elwang, *American Journal of Sociology* 60 (May 1955) 1–13. Compare John Dewey's similar but more reductivist notion of natural piety in *A Common Faith* (New Haven: Yale University Press, 1934) 25ff.

3. Albert Ellis, "The Case against Religion: A Psychotherapist's View," *Counseling and Psychotherapy*, ed. Ben Ard (Palo Alto, Cal.: Science and Behavior Books, 1966) 270–82.

4. "Nadine Gordimer," *Writers at Work: The Paris Review Interviews*, ed. George Plimpton (New York: Viking Press, 1984) 6: 269–70.

5. Annie Dillard, *An American Childhood* (New York: Harper and Row, 1987) 133.

6. Cf. the following selected passages in context: "Declaration on Religious Freedom," pars. 1–8; "Declaration on the Relationship of the Church to Non-Christian Religions," pars. 1–2, 5; "Dogmatic Constitution on the Church," par. 16; and "Pastoral Constitution on the Church in the Modern World," par. 79, in *Documents of Vatican II*, ed. Walter Abbott, S.J., Joseph Gallagher (New York: Guild Press, 1966).

7. For the text of Supreme Court Decision *U.S. versus Seeger*, see *United States Reports* 380 (1965) 163–93. For invaluable legal background and case summaries, I am indebted to the editors' introductory essay, "Conscientious Objectors," *Vanderbilt Law Review* (June 1965) 1564–73; and Robert Rabin, "When Is a Religious Belief Religious? United States vs. Seeger and the Scope of Free Exercise," *Cornell Law Review* 51 (1965–6) 231–49.

Chapter 2. Sacred Inside, Sacred Outside *(pp. 13–28)*

1. Note the basis and illustration of Common Prayer in David Yaego, "Meditation and Self-Examination: Reflections on Spirituality," *Dialog 21* (Summer 1982) 188.

2. Norman Brown, *Love's Body* (New York: Vintage Books, 1966) 222. For a further critique against literalist interpretation of the symbol, see Mircea Eliade, *Images and Symbols,* tr. Philip Mairet (New York: Sheed and Ward, 1961) 16.

3. Mary Collins, O.S.B., "Meditation on the Word's Meaning," *How Do I Pray?* ed. Robert Heyer (New York: Paulist Press, 1977) 64–66.

4. Hugh Nissenson, "The Blessing," *The Elephant and My Jewish Problem* (New York: Harper and Row, 1988) 1–10.

5. Gayle Baney Whittier, "Lost Time Accident," *Pushcart Prize,* ed. Bill Henderson (Yonkers, N.Y.: Pushcart Press, 1981) 6:29–49.

6. George Carlin, "Backstage," *Once a Catholic,* ed. Peter Occiogroso (Boston: Houghton Mifflin, 1987) 224–25.

7. Chingiz Aitmatov, *The Place of the Skull,* tr. Natasha Ward (New York: Grove Press, 1989) 53.

Chapter 3. An Imagination of the Sacred *(pp. 29–45)*

1. The results of this visualization exercise are reported in John Allan, *Inscapes of the Child's World: Jungian Counseling in Schools and Clinics* (Dallas: Spring Publications, 1988) 83–92. Also note specific cases of a harmful alliance between the God-image and parental image in Ana-Maria Rizzuto, *The Birth of the Living God* (Chicago: University of Chicago Press, 1979).

2. Cf. the survey of recent findings in Carl Roberts, "Imagining God: Who Is Created in Whose Image?" *Review of Religious Research* 30 (June 1989) 375–86; and the National Opinion Research Center statistics on image preferences in Andrew Greeley, *Religious Change in America* (Cambridge, Mass: Harvard University Press, 1989) 97ff. See the Rorschach conjectures in Peter Homans, "Toward a Psychology of Religion: By Way of Freud and Tillich," *The Dialogue between Theology and Psychology,* ed. Homans (Chicago: University of Chicago Press, 1968) 78ff.

3. See "Letters from the Earth," "Letters to the Earth," and other religious satire in Mark Twain, *Letters from the Earth,* ed. Bernard De Voto (New York: Harper and Row, 1974).

4. Tetsuo Yamaori, "The Metamorphosis of Ancestors," *Japan Quarterly* 33 (1986) 50–53.

5. My usage here is based on insightful discussions of "mesocosm" or "excluded middle" in David Augsburger, *Pastoral Counseling Across Cultures* (Philadelphia: Westminster Press, 1986) 33–35.

6. See William Christian, Jr., "The Spanish Shrine," *Numen* 24 (1977) 72–78.

7. Cf. the Walcott interview in *Writers at Work: The Paris Review Interviews,* ed. George Plimpton (New York: Viking Press, 1988) 8:272–76.

8. For sources and discussion of the Satan myth, see Vytautas Kavolis, "Civilizational Models of Evil," *Evil: Self and Culture,* ed. Marie Nelson and Michael Eigen (New York: Human Sciences Press, 1984) 17–35.

9. See Rollo May, ''Psychotherapy and the Daimonic,'' *Myths, Dreams, and Religion,* ed. Joseph Campbell (New York: Dutton, 1970) 196, 200–1.

10. Cf. the abbreviated version of this text in *Buddhist Scriptures,* ed. and tr. Edward Conze (Baltimore: Penguin Books, 1969) 229–30.

Chapter 4. The Way and Its Detours *(pp. 46–63)*

1. For a development of this position, see Ernest Becker, *The Denial of Death* (New York: Free Press, 1973) 66, 57f.; and Stanley Leavy, *In the Image of God: A Psychoanalyst's View* (New Haven: Yale University Press, 1988) 52f.

2. Freud, *Civilization and Its Discontents,* Standard Edition, tr. James Strachey (London: Hogarth Press, 1960) 21:144f. Subsequent Freud quotations will refer to the Standard Edition, unless otherwise indicated.

3. Lisa Wiley, ''Voices Calling (1955),'' *A Mad People's History of Madness,* ed. Dale Peterson (Pittsburgh: University of Pittsburgh Press, 1982) 271–83. Compare her account with the famous case from R. D. Laing, ''The Ghost of the Weed Garden: A Study of a Chronic Schizophrenic,'' *The Divided Self* (Baltimore: Penguin Books, 1965) 178–205.

4. Joseph Campbell, ''Schizophrenia: The Inward Journey,'' *Myths To Live By* (New York: Viking Press, 1972) 201–32. Cf. the development of these themes in my ''Primal Hunt,'' *Eight Sacred Horizons: The Religious Imagination East and West* (New York: Macmillan, 1985) 1–23. Also see Raymond Prince and Charles Savage, ''Mystical States and the Concept of Regression,'' and Kenneth Wapnick, ''Mysticism and Schizophrenia,'' *The Highest State of Consciousness,* ed. John White (Garden City, N.Y.: Anchor Books, 1972) 114–34, 153–74.

5. For illustrations of various healing rites, including ceremonies of closure, see Raymond Prince, ''Indigenous Yoruba Psychiatry,'' *Magic, Faith, and Healing,* ed. Ari Kiev (New York: Free Press, 1964) 84–121.

6. Sri Ramakrishna, *The Gospel of Sri Ramakrishna,* ed. and tr. Nikhilananda (New York: Ramakrishna-Vivekananda Center, 1942) 66.

7. Gregory Bateson, ''Introduction,'' *Perceval's Narrative: A Patient's Account of His Psychosis, 1830–1832,* ed. Bateson (Stanford, Calif.: Stanford University Press, 1961) xiv.

8. Joanne Greenberg (Hannah Green), *I Never Promised You a Rose Garden* (New York: Holt, Rinehart and Winston, 1964) 212, 46, 240; Hilde Bruch, transcriber of the taped lecture, ''Frieda Fromm-Reichmann Discusses the 'Rose Garden' Case,'' *Psychiatry* 45 (May 1982) 128–36. Also note the resourceful detective work about Greenberg's Hannah Green pseudonym in Peterson, 284–88.

9. William James, *Varieties of Religious Experience* (New York: Mentor Books, 1958) 326.

10. Peter Shaffer, *Equus* (New York: Avon Books, 1974) 123–24.

11. Cf. the context in Carl Jung, *Two Essays on Analytical Psychology,* tr. R. F. C. Hull (New York: Meridian Books, 1956) 176.

12. Joanne Greenberg, ''Palimpsest,'' *High Crimes and Misdemeanors* (New York: Holt, Rinehart and Winston, 1979) 105, 112–13.

13. Cf. Charles Morris, *Paths of Life: Preface to a World Religion* (Chicago: University of Chicago Press, 1973) 33–34. The notion of an evolving repertoire of symptoms is developed persuasively in Edward Shorter, "Paralysis: The Rise and Fall of a 'Hysterical' Symptom," *Journal of Social History* 19 (Summer 1986) 549–82.

14. This threefold Jewish typology is exemplified by Robert Cohn, "Sainthood on the Periphery: The Case of Judaism," *Sainthood: Its Manifestations in World Religions,* eds. Richard Kieckhefer and George Bond (Berkeley: University of California Press, 1988) 59–65. Notice other comparable typologies cited in Morris, *Varieties of Human Value* (Chicago: University of Chicago Press, 1956).

15. Ruth Prawer Jhabvala, "Two More under the Indian Sun," *Out of India* (New York: Morrow, 1986) 188, 197.

16. Kalidas Bhattacharyya, for example, rejects a comprehensive *samuccaya marga.* Note sources and rebuttal in my *Eight Sacred Horizons,* 64, 61–70.

17. Freud, "Libidinal Types" [1931], *Sigmund Freud: Character and culture,* ed. Philip Rieff, tr. Joan Riviere (New York: Collier Books, 1963) 213.

Chapter 5. Way of Action *(pp. 64–79)*

1. Cf. the extract from Gandhi's commentary on the Bhagavad Gita in *Gandhi: Selected Writings,* ed. Ronald Duncan (New York: Harper and Row, 1972) 33–39. Note the Gandhi and Mounier parallels in Emmanuel Mounier, *The Character of Man,* tr. Cynthia Rowland (London: Rockliff, 1956) 155, 140–41, 160–63.

2. Compare the resourceful discussion of this dilemma in Eleonore Stump, "Petitionary Prayer," *American Philosophical Quarterly* 16 (April 1979) 81–91; Donald Capps, "The Psychology of Petitionary Prayer," *Theology Today* 39 (July 1982) 130–41; and William Rogers, "Dependence and Counterdependency in Psychoanalysis and Religious Faith," *Zygon* 9:3 (September 1974) 190–201.

3. Excerpts from the two extended inscriptions are cited in Emanuel Sarkisyanz, *Buddhist Backgrounds of the Burmese Revolution* (The Hague: Nijhoff, 1965) 71–72.

4. Cf. Reinhold Niebuhr, *Moral Man and Immoral Society* (New York: Scribners, 1932) 102, 42–43, 64, including the President McKinley interview, cited above.

5. See *A Testament of Hope: Essential Writings of Martin Luther King, Jr.,* ed. James Washington (New York: Harper and Row, 1986) 259–67.

6. This phenomenon is documented in Ronald Enroth, "Terry Cole Whittaker Uses Television to Advance Her Own Version of the Gospel," *Christianity Today* 28 (September 21, 1984) 73–75; Jeffrey Haddon and Anson Shupe, "Televangelism in America," *Social Compass* 34 (1987) 61–74; and Michael Harris, "Heresy on the Airwaves," *Time* (March 5, 1990) 62.

7. Compare the resourceful description of the paranoid style in David Shapiro, *Neurotic Styles* (New York: Basic Books, 1965) 101–7. My approach follows Shapiro's distinction between neurosis and neurotic style, between symptom and trait, especially in paranoid and obsessive situations.

8. For example, Sun Tzu is cited repeatedly in a Swedish best-seller, Robert Duro's *Winning the Marketing War: A Practical Guide to Competitive Advantage,* tr. Tim Crosfield (New York: Wiley, 1989) 5, 81–83.

9. See the Mormon sources and overriding thesis in Laurence Moore, *Religious Outsiders and the Making of Americans* (New York: Oxford University Press, 1986) 34–35, 13; and the Nichiren background in Masaharu Anesaki, *Nichiren: The Buddhist Prophet* (Gloucester, Mass.: Peter Smith, 1966, 1916) 90, 119.

10. Cf. varied source materials amassed by a hostile Robertson ex-disciple, claiming his own liberation "from the cultic chains of fundamentalism to freedom of reason," in Gerard Straub, "Blowing the Whistle on Pat Robertson," *Humanist* (May 1988) 5–12, 36.

11. For the documentation on Columbus' religious version of his mission, see Mircea Eliade, *The Quest: History and Meaning in Religion* (Chicago: University of Chicago Press, 1969) 90–91. For evidence of President Reagan's beliefs about an Armageddon nuclear war, see John Herbers, "Armageddon View Prompts a Debate," *New York Times* (October 25, 1984) 1, 13.

12. Cf. the alleged interview with Dr. Jordan in Michael D'Antonio, *Fall from Grace: The failed Crusade of the Christian Right* (New York: Farrar, Straus, Giroux, 1989) 144.

13. Cf. Shapiro, 51–52. For an informed description of the obsessive style, see 23–53; and his *Autonomy and Rigid Character* (Basic Books, 1981). Also see Jerrold Pollak, "Relationship of Obsessive-Compulsive Personality to Obsessive-Compulsive Disorder: A Review of the Literature," *Journal of Psychology* 12 (March 1987) 137–48.

14. Note the oversimplified version of a univocal "Catholic approach" to scrupulosity, compared to a traditional rabbinic treatment, in Judith Rapoport, *The Boy Who Couldn't Stop Washing: The Experience and Treatment of Obsessive-Compulsive Disorder* (New York: Dutton, 1989) 235–44. Rapoport favors a combined drug and behavioral conditioning program for clinical obsessive-compulsive disorders. Against classical authoritarian treatments, see the nuanced psychological critique over thirty years ago in George Hagmaier, C.S.P., and Robert Gleason, S.J., *Counselling the Catholic: Modern Techniques and Emotional Conflicts* (New York: Sheed and Ward, 1959) 145–73.

15. Harry Taylor, *The Divorce Sonnets* (Baton Rouge: Louisiana State University Press, 1984) 66.

16. Emmanuel Mounier, *Personalism,* tr. Philip Mairet (New York: Grove Press, 1952) 93.

Chapter 6. Way of Affectivity *(pp. 80–94)*

1. Edward Morgan Forster, *Passage to India* (New York: Harcourt, Brace and World, 1924) 245.

2. Ruth Prawer Jhabvala, "The Widow," *Out of India* (New York: Morrow, 1986) 39–56.

3. See Becker, 167–68, 152ff., 182ff.

4. Cf. Richard Kalish, "Of Children and Grandfathers: A Speculative Essay on Dependency," *The Dependencies of Old People,* ed. Kalish (Ann Arbor: University of Michigan Press, 1969) 73–83; and Willard Gaylin, "In the beginning: Helpless and Dependent," *Doing Good: The Limits of Benevolence,* eds. Gaylin and others (New York: Pantheon Books, 1978) 1–38.

5. Erik Erikson, *Young Man Luther: A Study in Psychoanalysis and History* (New York: Norton, 1962) 255, 118–19.

6. Takeo Doi, *The Anatomy of Dependence,* tr. John Bester (New York: Kodansha International, 1973) 63, 57; and "Amae: A Key Concept for Understanding Japanese Personality Structure," in *Japanese Culture: Its Development and Characteristics,* eds. Robert Smith and Richard Beardsley (Chicago: Aldine, 1962) 132–39. The Mahler citation occurs in Jarl Dyrud, "The Contemporary Debate on 'Narcissism' as a Dominant Cultural Type," *The Challenge of Psychology To Faith,* eds. Steven Kepnes and David Tracy (New York: Seabury Press, 1982) 71. See the review of recent Attachment Theory in Robert Karen, "Becoming Attached," *Atlantic Monthly* (February 1990) 35–50, 63–82.

7. Freud, "Libidinal Types," 211.

8. For this example and other case parallels, see *Adult Children of Alcoholics Remember,* ed. Nelson Hayes (New York: Harmony Books, 1989) 74, 126, 60.

9. Cf. *United States versus Ballard* (1944), cited in William Shepherd, "The Prosecutor's Reach: Legal Issues Stemming from the New Religious Movements," *JAAR* 50 (1982) 187–88. For useful descriptive bibliography on the cult phenomenon, see Thomas Robbins, "New Religious Movement, Brainwashing, and Deprogramming—The View from the Law Journals: A Review Essay and Survey," *Religious Studies Review* 2:4 (October 1985) 361–70; and John Saliba, S.J., *Psychiatry and the Cults: An Annotated Bibliography* (New York: Garland, 1987).

10 Karen Horney, *Neurosis and Human Growth* (New York: Norton, 1950) 221, 223, 219. For extended descriptions of morbid dependency and compliance, see 214–58, and also *Our Inner Conflicts* (New York: Norton, 1945) 48–62.

11. Cf. Phil. 2:7; Satapatha Brahmana 13:1; 6:1,2,12-13. Note evidence on the Shaivite poet mystics in Carl Olson, "The Shaiva Mystic, Self Sacrifice, and Creativity," *Religion* 10 (Spring 1980) 31–40.

12. Though the interpretation is my own, the source material on medieval anorexics is drawn mostly from Rudolph Bell's persuasive study, *Holy Anorexia* (Chicago: University of Chicago Press, 1985). Yet see Carolyn Bynum's critique of Bell in *Fragmentation and Redemption: Essays on Gender and the Human Body in Medieval Religion* (Cambridge, Mass.: Zone Books, 1991). For analysis of crucial genre expectations in medieval hagiography, see Thomas Heffernon, *Sacred Biography: Saints and Their Biographers in the Middle Ages* (New York: Oxford University Press, 1988). The methodology implied in Bell's later study is expounded more clearly in Donald Weinstein and Rudolph Bell, *Saints and Society: The two Worlds of Western Christendom, 1000–1700* (Chicago: University of Chicago Press, 1982).

13. Cf. Jules Bemporad and others, "Hysteria, Anorexia and the Culture of Self-Denial," *Psychiatry* 51 (February 1988) 96–102. The family psychology and bourgeois era context of hysteria are well outlined in Richard Sennett, *The Fall of Public Man* (New York: Knopf, 1977) 182f., 324f.

14. Cf. her letter to Diodat Roche, where Weil mentions conscious Albigensian affinities, in *Simone Weil: Seventy Letters,* ed. and tr. Richard Rees (New York: Oxford University Press, 1965) 129–31. See also her *First and Last Notebooks* (New York: Oxford University Press, 1970).

15. I am indebted to Robert Coles, *Simone Weil: A Modern Pilgrimage* (Reading, Mass.: Addison-Wesley, 1987), especially the second chapter, entitled "Her Hunger," 23–41, 131-32, for his psychological insight, including the dialogue with Anna Freud. More benign than my own, his final appraisal downplays Weil's self-destructive eccentricities within the generous perspective of a book-length portrait.

16. Cf. her letter to Joe Bousquet (1942) in *Seventy Letters,* 136–42.

Chapter 7. Way of Contemplation *(pp. 95–110)*

1. Kenneth Kaunda, *A Humanist in Africa: Letters to Colin M. Morris* (Nashville: Abingdon Press, 1966) 29–30.

2. Thomas Williams, "Goose Pond," in *Writer's Choice,* ed. Rust Hills (New York: David McKay, 1974) 197–411. Note Williams' evocative introductory comments for this edition, giving the story genesis. For further discussion of this missing inward dimension, see Raimundo Panikkar, "The Contemplative Mood: A Challenge to Modernity," *Cross Currents* (Fall 1981) 261–72.

3. See the Letter of February 22nd, 1923 in *Letters of Rainer Maria Rilke: 1892–1926,* eds. and trs. Jane Greene and Mary Norton (New York: Norton, 1948) II.

4. Doris Donnelly, "A Child Shall Lead Them," Heyer 1–3.

5. Cf. the Winnicott citations and discussion in Paul Pruyser, "Psychological Roots and Branches of Belief," *Pastoral Psychology* 28 (Fall 1979) 8–20; and Diane Jonte-Pace, "Object Relations Theory, Mothering, and Religion: Toward a Feminist Psychology of Religion," *Horizons* 14 (February 1987) 310–27. See also Erik Erikson, "Play and Actuality," *A Way of Looking at Things: Selected Papers of Erik H. Erikson, 1930–1985,* ed. Stephen Schlein (New York: Norton, 1987) 335–36.

6. Heinz Kohut, *The Search for the Self: Selected Writings of Heinz Kohut, 1950–1978,* ed. Paul Ornstein (New York: International Universities Press, 1978) I:455. And compare the abbreviated case studies of neurotic resignation and detachment in Horney, *Neurosis,* 259–90.

7. John Courtney Murray, S.J., "The Danger of the Vows," *Woodstock Letters* (Fall 1967) 421.

8. Evelyn Waugh, *The Ordeal of Gilbert Pinfold* (London: Chapman and Hall, 1957) 6–8. For evidence of progressive social and spiritual isolation in

Waugh himself, see Jeffrey Heath, *The Picturesque Prison: Evelyn Waugh and His Writing* (Kingston, Ontario: McGill-Queen's University Press, 1982) 259–74.

9. Cf. the case illustrations from Morita, Naikan, Seiza, Shadan, and Zen therapies in David Reynolds, *The Quiet Therapies: Japanese Pathways to Personal Growth* (Honolulu: University of Hawaii Press, 1980).

10. John of the Cross, *Dark Night of the Soul*, tr. Allison Peers (Garden City, N.Y.: Image Books, 1959) 54–55. John's distinction between God's grace itself and an individual's psychological experience of its presence dominates Cardinal Ratzinger's censures against the Christian's uncritical adoption of Eastern prayer techniques and attitudes. Cf. the Doctrinal Congregation's letter, "Some Aspects of Christian Meditation," *Origins* 19 (December 28, 1989) 492–98, especially pars. 9, 12, 16, 26–28.

11. Alan Watts, "Beat Zen, Square Zen, Zen," *This Is It: And Other Essays on Zen and Spiritual Experience* (New York: Pantheon Books, 1960) 101, 103–6, 91–94. Watts cites a description by John Clelland-Holmes.

12. Cf. Peter Marin, "Spiritual Obedience," *Harper's* 258 (February 1979) 47.

13. Abraham Maslow, *Religions, Values, and Peak-Experiences,* 2nd ed. (New York: Viking Press, 1970) 25, vii, viii–xi. His new preface corrects the earlier edition's lopsided apologia for individual experience almost as an end in itself, abandoning any trace of the Religious Establishment.

14. John of the Cross, 54–55, 68. And note an examination of the *makyo* concept in William Johnston, S.J., *Being in Love: The Practice of Christian Prayer* (New York: Harper and Row, 1989) 84.

15. For instance, compare the varied approaches in *Culture and Depression: Studies in the Anthropology and Cross-Cultural Psychiatry of Affect and Disorder,* eds. Arthur Kleinman and Byron Good (Berkeley: University of California Press, 1985).

16. Carl Jung, *Analytical Psychology: Its Theory and Practice* (New York: Vintage Books, 1970) 116.

17. See a summary of the traditional tantric doctrine in Haridas Chaudhuri, "Yoga Psychology," *Transpersonal Psychologies,* ed. Charles Tart (Harper and Row, 1975) 231–80.

Chapter 8. The Healing Spirit *(pp. 111–129)*

1. John Updike, *Roger's Version* (New York: Knopf, 1987) 32.

2. Note my discussion of the nganga and shaman in *Eight Sacred Horizons,* 7–12.

3. Njabulo Ndebele, "The Prophetess," *Fools and Other Stories* (Harlow, Essex: Longman, 1985) 30–52.

4. Freud, "The Psychogenesis of a Case of Homosexuality in a Woman," 18:150.

5. Erich Fromm, D. T. Suzuki, and Richard De Martino, *Zen Buddhism and Psychoanalysis* (New York: Harper and Row, 1960) 85–86.

6. Freud, "Analysis Terminable and Interminable," 23:249.

7. This overextension of role is well exemplified by Thomas Maeder, ''Wounded Healers,'' *Atlantic Monthly* (January 1989) 37–47.

8. Lynne Sharon Schwartz, ''The Age of Analysis,'' *Acquainted with the Night* (New York: Harper and Row, 1984) 1-37.

9. Jung, *Analytical Psychology,* 171–72.

10. Cf. The Manu citation in J. S. Neki, ''Guru-Chela Relationship: The Possibility of a Therapeutic Paradigm,'' *American Journal of Orthopsychiatry* 43 (1973) 757. See also R. Ravindra, ''Is Religion Psychotherapy? An Indian View,'' *Religious Studies* 14 (September 1978) 389–97. For sample Hindu critiques of guru distortion, see my *Eight Sacred Horizons,* 59–61. The Tantric Buddhist version can be found in Chogyam Trungpa, *Cutting Through Spiritual Materialism* (Berkeley: Shambhala Press, 1987) 42–45.

11. See the editors, ''Monks of Cuernavaca Using Psychoanalysis,'' *Catholic Mind* (September 1967) 5–8, for extracts from Lemercier's statement of June 12, responding to a Vatican censure. See also Louis Allen, ''The Rule of Saint Freud,'' *New Blackfriars* 48 (September 9, 1967) 641–49.

12. Despite his earlier seminary training, Carl Rogers apparently does not recognize the theological premises that underly his psychology. Note the debate with Bernard Loomer, Walter Horton, and Hans Hofmann in Carl Rogers, ''Reinhold Niebuhr's *The Self and the Dramas of History:* A Criticism,'' *Pastoral Psychology* 9 (June 1958) 15–28. See an extended critique of the Third Force Psychologists' most familiar axioms in Don Browning, *Religious Thought and the Modern Psychologies* (Philadelphia: Fortress Press, 1987) 59–93.

13. Cf. further criticisms by Judd Marmor, ''The Psychoanalyst as a Person,'' *American Journal of Psychoanalysis* 37 (1977) 275–84; and Robert Coles, ''Psychology As Faith,'' *Theology Today* (April 1985) 69–71. See the useful discussion and bibliography in Peter Breggin, ''Psychotherapy as Applied Ethics,'' *Psychiatry* 34 (February 1971) 59–74; and Robert Moore, ''Contemporary Psychotherapy as Ritual Process: An Initial Reconnaissance,'' *Zygon* 18:3 (September 1983) 283–94.

14. See the review of empathy theories and bibliography in Russell Meares, ''Keats and the *Impersonal* Therapist: A Note on Empathy and the Therapeutic Screen,'' *Psychiatry* 46 (February 1983) 73–82; and Howard Book, ''Empathy: Misconceptions and Misuses in Psychotherapy,'' *American Journal of Psychiatry* 145:4 (April 1988) 420–24 [with reponses and rebuttal in 146:3 (March 1989) 413–14.].

15. *Psychoanalysis and Faith: The Letters of Sigmund Freud and Oskar Pfister,* eds. Heinrich Meng and Ernst Freud, tr. Eric Mosbacher (New York: Basic Books, 1963) 113.

16. Robert Lindner, *The Fifty-Minute Hour* (New York: Bantam Books, 1971) 156–207.

17. Note the current attempts to stress empathic communication throughout the training of young physicians, as documented in Edward Krupat, ''A Delicate Imbalance,'' *Psychology Today* (November 1986) 22–26; and Arthur Kleinman, *The Illness Narratives: Suffering, Healing, and the Human Condition* (New York: Basic Books, 1988).

18. William Styron, ''Darkness Visible,'' *Vanity Fair* 62:2 (December 1989) 285.

19. Cf. Waud Kracke, ''Encounter with Other Cultures: Psychological and Epistemological Aspects,'' *Ethos* 15 (1987) 58–81; and Joseph Tobin, ''(Counter)transference and Failure in Intercultural Therapy,'' *Ethos* 14 (1986) 120–43.

20. Margaret Mead, *Blackberry Winter: My Earliest Years* (New York: Morrow, 1972) 281–82.

21. Carl Jung, ''Psychotherapy and a Philosophy of Life,'' *Collected Works*, tr. R. F. C. Hull (Princeton: Princeton University Press, 1966) 83.

Bibliography

Abbott, Walter, S.J., ed. *Documents of Vatican II.* Tr. Joseph Gallagher New York: Guild Press, 1966.

Aitmatov, Chingiz. *The Place of the Skull.* Tr. Natasha Ward. New York: Grove Press, 1989.

Allan, John. *Inscapes of the Child's World: Jungian Counseling in Schools and Clinics.* Dallas: Spring Publications, 1988.

Allen, Louis. "The Rule of Saint Freud." *New Blackfriars* 48 (September 9, 1967) 641–49.

Anesaki, Masaharu. *Nichiren: The Buddhist Prophet.* Gloucester, Mass.: Peter Smith, 1966, 1916.

Ard, Ben, ed. *Counseling and Psychotherapy.* Palo Alto: Science and Behavior Books, 1966.

Augsburger, David. *Pastoral Counseling Across Cultures.* Philadelphia: Westminster Press, 1986.

Bateson, Gregory, ed. *Perceval's Narrative: A Patient's Account of His Psychosis, 1830–1832.* Stanford: Stanford University Press, 1961.

Becker, Ernest. *The Denial of Death.* New York: Free Press, 1973.

Bell, Rudolph. *Holy Anorexia.* Chicago: University of Chicago Press, 1985.

Bemporad, Jules, and others. "Hysteria, Anorexia and the Culture of Self-Denial." *Psychiatry* 51 (February 1988) 96–102.

Book, Howard. "Empathy: Misconceptions and Misuses in Psychotherapy." *American Journal of Psychiatry* 145:4 (April 1988) 420–24, and 146:3 (March 1989) 413–14.

Breggin, Peter. "Psychotherapy As Applied Ethics," *Psychiatry* 34 (February 1971) 59–74.

Brown, Norman. *Love's Body.* New York: Vintage Books, 1966.

Browning, Don. *Religious Thought and the Modern Psychologies.* Philadelphia: Fortress Press, 1987.

Bruch, Hilde, transcriber. "Frieda Fromm-Reichmann Discusses the 'Rose Garden' Case." *Psychiatry* 45 (May 1982), 128–36.

Burridge, Kenelm. *Encountering Aborigines: A Case Study.* New York: Pergamon Press, 1973.

Bynum, Carolyn. *Fragmentation and Redemption: Essays on Gender and the Human Body in Medieval Religion.* Cambridge, Mass.: Zone Books, 1991.

Campbell, Joseph, ed. *Myths, Dreams, and Religion.* New York: Dutton, 1970.

———. *Myths to Live By.* New York: Viking Press, 1972.

Capps, Donald. "The Psychology of Petitionary Prayer." *Theology Today* 39 (July 1982) 130–41.

Christian, William, Jr. "The Spanish Shrine." *Numen* 24 (1977) 72–78.

Coles, Robert. "Psychology As Faith." *Theology Today* (April 1985) 69–71.

———. *Simone Weil: A Modern Pilgrimage.* Reading, Mass.: Addison-Wesley, 1987.

"Conscientious Objectors." *Vanderbilt Law Review* (June 1965) 1564–73.

Conze, Edward, ed. and tr. *Buddhist Scriptures.* Baltimore: Penguin Books, 1969.

D'Antonio, Michael. *Fall from Grace: The Failed Crusade of the Christian Right.* New York: Farrar, Straus, Giroux, 1989.

Dewey, John. *A Common Faith.* New Haven, Conn.: Yale University Press, 1934.

Dillard, Annie. *An American Childhood.* New York: Harper and Row, 1987.

Doi, Takeo. *The Anatomy of Dependence.* Tr. John Bester. New York: Kodansha International, 1973.

Duro, Robert. *Winning the Marketing War: A Practical Guide to Competitive Advantage.* Tr. Tim Crosfield. New York: Wiley, 1989.

Eliade, Mircea. *Images and Symbols.* Tr. Philip Mairet. New York: Sheed and Ward, 1961.

———. *The Quest: History and Meaning in Religion.* Chicago: University of Chicago Press, 1969.

Enroth, Ronald. "Terry Cole Whittaker Uses Television to Advance Her Own Version of the Gospel." *Christianity Today* 28 (September 21, 1984) 73–75.

Erikson, Erik. *Young Man Luther: A Study in Psychoanalysis and History.* New York: Norton, 1962.

———. *A Way of Looking at Things: Selected Papers of Erik H. Erikson, 1930–1985.* Ed. Stephen Schlein. New York: Norton, 1987.

Forster, Edward Morgan. *Passage to India.* New York: Harcourt, Brace and World, 1924.

Freud, Sigmund. *Psychoanalysis and Faith: The Letters of Sigmund Freud and Oskar Pfister*. Eds. Heinrich Meng and Ernst Freud, tr. Eric Mosbacher. New York: Basic Books, 1963.

________. *Sigmund Freud: Character and Culture*. Ed. Philip Rieff, tr. Joan Riviere. New York: Collier Books, 1963.

________. *Standard Edition of the Complete Psychological Works*. Ed. and tr. James Strachey. London: Hogarth Press, 1953–74.

Fromm, Erich, D. T. Suzuki, and Richard De Martino. *Zen Buddhism and Psychoanalysis*. New York: Harper and Row, 1960.

Gandhi, Mohandas. *Gandhi: Selected Writings*. Ed. Ronald Duncan. New York: Harper and Row, 1972.

Gaylin, Willard, and others. *The Limits of Benevolence*. New York: Pantheon Books, 1978.

Greeley, Andrew. *Religious Change in America*. Cambridge, Mass.: Harvard University Press, 1989.

Greenberg, Joanne. *High Crimes and Misdemeanors*. New York: Holt, Rinehart and Winston, 1979.

________. *I Never Promised You a Rose Garden*. New York: Holt, Rinehart and Winston, 1964.

Haddon, Jeffrey, and Anson Shupe. "Televangelism in America." *Social Compass* 34 (1987) 61–74.

Hagmaier, George, C.S.P., and Robert Gleason, S.J. *Counselling the Catholic: Modern Techniques and Emotional Conflicts*. New York: Sheed and Ward, 1959.

Harris, Michael. "Heresy on the Airwaves." *Time* (March 5, 1990) 62.

Hayes, Nelson, ed. *Adult Children of Alcoholics Remember*. New York: Harmony Books, 1989.

Heath, Jeffrey. *The Picturesque Prison: Evelyn Waugh and His Writing*. Kingston, Ontario: McGill-Queen's University Press, 1982.

Heffernon, Thomas. *Sacred Biography: Saints and Their Biographers in the Middle Ages*. New York: Oxford University Press, 1988.

Henderson, Bill, ed. *Pushcart Prize 6*. Yonkers, N.Y.: Pushcart Press, 1981.

Herbers, John. "Armageddon View Prompts a Debate." *New York Times* (October 25, 1984) 1, 13.

Heyer, Robert, ed. *How Do I Pray?* New York: Paulist Press, 1977.

Hills, Rust, ed. *Writer's Choice*. New York: David McKay, 1974.

Homans, Peter, ed. *The Dialogue between Theology and Psychology*. Chicago: University of Chicago Press, 1968.

Horney, Karen. *Neurosis and Human Growth*. New York: Norton, 1950.

________. *Our Inner Conflicts*. New York: Norton, 1945.

James, William. *Varieties of Religious Experience*. New York: Mentor Books, 1958.

Jhabvala, Ruth Prawer. *Out of India.* New York: Morrow, 1986.
John of the Cross. *Dark Night of the Soul.* Tr. Allison Peers. Garden City, N.Y.: Image Books, 1959.
Johnston, William, S.J. *Being in Love: The Practice of Christian Prayer.* New York: Harper and Row, 1989.
Jonte-Pace, Diane. "Object Relations Theory, Mothering, and Religion: Toward a Feminist Psychology of Religion." *Horizons* 14 (February 1987) 310–27.
Jung, Carl. *Analytical Psychology: Its Theory and Practice.* New York: Vintage Books, 1970.
________. *Collected Works.* Tr. R. F. C. Hull. Princeton, N.J.: Princeton University Press, 1953–.
________. *Two Essays on Analytical Psychology.* Tr. R. F. C. Hull. New York: Meridian Books, 1956.
Kalish, Richard, ed. *The Dependencies of Old People.* Ann Arbor: University of Michigan Press, 1969.
Karen, Robert. "Becoming Attached." *Atlantic Monthly* (February 1990) 35–50, 63–82.
Kaunda, Kenneth. *A Humanist in Africa: Letters to Colin M. Morris.* Nashville: Abingdon Press, 1966.
Kepnes, Steven, and David Tracy, eds. *The Challenge of Psychology to Faith.* New York: Seabury Press, 1982.
Kiekhefer, Richard, and George Bond, eds. *Sainthood: Its Manifestations in World Religions.* Berkeley: University of California Press, 1988.
Kiev, Ari, ed. *Magic, Faith, and Healing.* New York: Free Press, 1964.
King, Martin Luther, Jr. *A Testament of Hope: Essential Writings of Martin Luther King, Jr.* Ed. James Washington. New York: Harper and Row, 1986.
Kleinman, Arthur. *The Illness Narratives: Suffering, Healing, and the Human Condition.* New York: Basic Books, 1988.
Kleinman, Arthur, and Byron Good, eds. *Culture and Depression: Studies in the Anthropology and Cross-Cultural Psychiatry of Affect and Disorder.* Berkeley: University of California Press, 1985.
Kohut, Heinz. *The Search for the Self: Selected Writings of Heinz Kohut, 1950–1978.* Ed. Paul Ornstein. New York: International Universities Press, 1978.
Kracke, Waud. "Encounter with Other Cultures: Psychological and Epistemological Aspects." *Ethos* 15 (1987) 58–81.
Krupat, Edward. "A Delicate Imbalance." *Psychology Today* (November 1986) 22–26.
Laing, R. D. *The Divided Self.* Baltimore: Penguin Books, 1965.
Leavy, Stanley. *In the Image of God: A Psychoanalyst's View.* New Haven,

Conn.: Yale University Press, 1988.

Lindner, Robert. *The Fifty-Minute Hour.* New York: Bantam Books, 1971.

Maeder, Thomas. ''Wounded Healers.'' *Atlantic Monthly* (January 1989) 37–47.

Marin, Peter. ''Spiritual Obedience.'' *Harper's* 258 (February 1979) 43–58.

Marmor, Judd. ''The Psychoanalyst as a Person.'' *American Journal of Psychoanalysis* 37 (1977) 275–84.

Maslow, Abraham. *Religions, Values, and Peak-Experiences.* 2d ed. New York: Viking Press, 1970.

Mead, Margaret. *Blackberry Winter: My Earliest Years.* New York: Morrow, 1972.

Meares, Russell. Keats and the *Impersonal* Therapist: A Note on Empathy and the Therapeutic Screen.'' *Psychiatry* 46 (February 1983) 73–82.

''Monks of Cuernavaca Using Psychoanalysis.'' *Catholic Mind* (September 1967) 5–8.

Moore, Laurence. *Religious Outsiders and the Making of Americans.* New York: Oxford University Press, 1986.

Moore, Robert. ''Contemporary Psychotherapy As Ritual Process: An Initial Reconnaissance.'' *Zygon* 18:3 (September 1983) 283–94.

Morris, Charles. *Paths of Life: Preface to a World Religion.* Chicago: University of Chicago Press, 1973.

________. *Varieties of Human Value.* Chicago: University of Chicago Press, 1956.

Mounier, Emmanuel. *The Character of Man.* Tr. Cynthia Rowland. London: Rockliff, 1956.

________. *Personalism.* Trans. Philip Mairet. New York: Grove Press, 1952.

Murray, John Courtney, S.J. ''The Danger of the Vows.'' *Woodstock Letters* (Fall 1967) 421–27.

Ndebele, Njabulo. *Fools and Other Stories.* Harlow, Essex: Longman, 1985.

Neki, J. S. ''Guru-Chela Relationship: The Possibility of a Therapeutic Paradigm.'' *American Journal of Orthopsychiatry* 43 (1973) 755–66.

Nelson, Marie, and Michael Eigen, eds. *Evil: Self and Culture.* New York: Human Sciences Press, 1984.

Niebuhr, Reinhold. *Moral Man and Immoral Society.* New York: Scribners, 1932.

Nissenson, Hugh. *The Elephant and My Jewish Problem.* New York: Harper and Row, 1988.

Occiogroso, Peter, ed. *Once a Catholic.* Boston: Houghton Mifflin, 1987.

Olson, Carl. "The Shaiva Mystic, Self Sacrifice, and Creativity." *Religion* 10 (Spring 1980) 31–40.

Panikkar, Raimundo. "The Contemplative Mood: A Challenge to Modernity." *Cross Currents* (Fall 1981) 261–72.

Peterson, Dale, ed. *A Mad People's History of Madness.* Pittsburgh: University of Pittsburgh Press, 1982.

Plimpton, George, ed. *Writers at Work: The Paris Review Interviews.* New York: Viking Press, 1958–.

Pollak, Jerrold. "Relationship of Obsessive-Compulsive Personality to Obsessive-Compulsive Disorder: A Review of the Literature." *Journal of Psychology* 12 (March 1987) 137–48.

Pruyser, Paul. "Psychological Roots and Branches of Belief" *Pastoral Psychology* 28 (Fall 1979) 8–20.

Rabin, Robert. "When Is a Religious Belief Religious? United States vs. Seeger and the Scope of Free Exercise." *Cornell Law Review* 51 (1965–66) 231–49.

Ramakrishna, Sri. *The Gospel of Sri Ramakrishna.* Ed. and tr. Nikhilananda. New York: Ramakrishna-Vivekananda Center, 1942.

Rapoport, Judith. *The Boy Who Couldn't Stop Washing: The Experience and Treatment of Obsessive-Compulsive Disorder.* New York: Dutton, 1989.

Ratzinger, Joseph. "Some Aspects of Christian Meditation." *Origins* 19 (December 28, 1989) 492–98.

Ravindra, R. "Is Religion Psychotherapy? An Indian View." *Religious Studies* 14 (September 1978) 389–97.

Reynolds, David. *The Quiet Therapies: Japanese Pathways to Personal Growth.* Honolulu: University of Hawaii Press, 1980.

Rilke, Rainer Maria. *Letters of Rainer Maria Rilke: 1892-1926.* Eds. and trs. Jane Greene and Mary Norton. New York: Norton, 1948.

Rizzuto, Ana-Maria. *The Birth of the Living God.* Chicago: University of Chicago Press, 1979.

Robbins, Thomas. "New Religious Movement, Brainwashing, and Deprogramming—The View from the Law Journals: A Review Essay and Survey." *Religious Studies Review* 2:4 (October 1985) 361–70.

Roberts, Carl. "Imagining God: Who Is Created in Whose Image?" *Review of Religious Research* 30 (June 1989) 375–86.

Rogers, Carl. "Reinhold Niebuhr's *The Self and the Dramas of History:* A Criticism." *Pastoral Psychology* 9 (June 1958) 15–28.

Rogers, William. "Dependence and Counterdependency in Psychoanalysis and Religious Faith." *Zygon* 9:3 (September 1974) 190–201.

Ruland, Vernon, S.J. *Eight Sacred Horizons: The Religious Imagination East and West.* New York: Macmillan, 1985.

Saliba, John, S.J. *Psychiatry and the Cults: An Annotated Bibliography.* New York: Garland, 1987.

Sarkisyanz, Emanuel. *Buddhist Backgrounds of the Burmese Revolution.* The Hague: Nijhoff, 1965.

Schlitzer, Albert, C.S.C., ed. *The Spirit and Power of Christian Secularity.* Notre Dame, Ind.: University of Notre Dame Press, 1969.

Schwartz, Lynne Sharon. *Acquainted with the Night.* New York: Harper and Row, 1984.

Sennett, Richard. *The Fall of Public Man.* New York: Knopf, 1977.

Shaffer, Peter. *Equus.* New York: Avon Books, 1974.

Shapiro, David. *Autonomy and Rigid Character.* Basic Books, 1981.

________. *Neurotic Styles.* New York: Basic Books, 1965.

Shepherd, William. ''The Prosecutor's Reach: Legal Issues Stemming from the New Religious Movements.'' *JAAR* 50 (1982) 187–214.

Shorter, Edward. ''Paralysis: The Rise and Fall of a 'Hysterical' Symptom.'' *Journal of Social History* 19 (Summer 1986) 549–82.

Simmel, Georg. ''A Contribution to the Sociology of Religion.'' Tr. W. W. Elwang. *American Journal of Sociology* 60 (May 1955) 1–13.

Smith, Robert, and Richard Beardsley, eds. *Japanese Culture: Its Development and Characteristics.* Chicago: Aldine, 1962.

Straub, Gerard. ''Blowing the Whistle on Pat Robertson.'' *Humanist* (May 1988) 5–12, 36.

Stump, Eleonore. ''Petitionary Prayer.'' *American Philosophical Quarterly* 16 (April 1979) 81–91.

Styron, William. ''Darkness Visible.'' *Vanity Fair* 62:2 (December 1989) 212–24, 286–87.

Tart, Charles, ed. *Transpersonal Psychologies.* New York: Harper and Row, 1975.

Taylor, Harry. *The Divorce Sonnets.* Baton Rouge, La.: Louisiana State University Press, 1984.

Tobin, Joseph. ''(Counter)transference and Failure in Intercultural Therapy.'' *Ethos* 14 (1986) 120–43.

Trungpa, Chogyam. *Cutting through Spiritual Materialism.* Berkeley: Shambhala Press, 1987.

Twain, Mark. *Letters from the Earth.* Ed. Bernard De Voto. New York: Harper and Row, 1974.

''U.S. versus Seeger.'' *United States Reports* 380 (1965) 163–93.

Updike, John. *Roger's Version.* New York: Knopf, 1987.

Watts, Alan. *This Is It: And Other Essays on Zen and Spiritual Experience.* New York: Pantheon Books, 1960.

Waugh, Evelyn. *The Ordeal of Gilbert Pinfold.* London: Chapman and Hall, 1957.

Weil, Simone. *First and Last Notebooks.* Tr. Richard Rees. New York: Oxford University Press, 1970.

________. *Simone Weil: Seventy Letters.* Ed. and tr. Richard Rees. New York: Oxford University Press, 1965.

Weinstein, Donald, and Rudolph Bell. *Saints and Society: The Two Worlds of Western Christendom, 1000–1700.* Chicago: University of Chicago Press, 1982.

White, John, ed. *The Highest State of Consciousness.* Garden City, N.Y.: Anchor Books, 1972.

Yaego, David. ''Meditation and Self-Examination: Reflections on Spirituality.'' *Dialog* 21 (Summer 1982) 184–89.

Yamaori, Tetsuo. ''The Metamorphosis of Ancestors.'' *Japan Quarterly* 33 (1986) 50–53.

Index